"I've spent a lifetime in athletics b[...] glory of God in training the body [...] Scripture's!) of a vigorous life to t[...] walk into the gym differently this [...]
**Rick Barnes**, Head Basketball [...]

"In *A Little Theology of Exercise*, David Mathis has written a unique and timely book to help Christians think spiritually about exercise in a sedentary age. Specifically, he answers the question 'How can the joy of exercise serve joy in God?' David skillfully avoids the pitfalls of either idolizing or ignoring the body by presenting a theology of the body from creation to fall to redemption to glorification. And so he presents a short theological manual packed with godly motivations for the use of the body to the glory of God. This book will challenge you, but it will also change the way you think about spiritual pleasure and physical exercise."
**Gavin Peacock**, former professional footballer; Locum Pastor, Bethersden Baptist Church, UK; author, *A Greater Glory: From Pitch to Pulpit*

"'Little' is putting it lightly. David Mathis's *A Little Theology of Exercise* is a work for such a time as this. Despite spending more on being healthy than ever before, Americans live in a largely sedentary culture and face a growing obesity epidemic. Given that context, his work strikes a necessary balance between convicting admonitions and instructive exhortations. Filled with biblical truths that highlight the remarkably designed human body with its God-given capacity for exercise, the book provides an excellent theological framework by which Christians should engage in exercise. I am especially grateful for David's enlightening, embodied approach to exercise, one that recognizes the value of both soul and body health. Whether you exercise five days a week or five days a year, if you desire to glorify God with your life—with your body—I highly recommend his book."
**Lainey Greer**, Founder, Your Body Matters; author, *Embodied Holiness: The Biblical Call to Bodily Care*

"David Mathis offers a biblical vision for physical exercise that reveals the deep connection between body and soul. Rather than viewing exercise as a secular activity or a means of self-improvement, Mathis reframes it as a God-given gift that can enhance joy in Christ to the glory of God. Whether you're an athlete or someone simply seeking a more faithful approach to fitness, this book will challenge and encourage you."

**Jeremy Treat**, Pastor for Preaching and Vision, Reality LA, Los Angeles, California; Professor of Theology, Biola University; author, *The Crucified King*; *Seek First*; *The Atonement*; and *Renewal in Christ*

"There is a growing obsession on social media with health matters. Apparently, everyone has a health tip! There's a type of idolatry and legalism that creeps into such discussions. The solution isn't to avoid these worthwhile topics but to look at them as Christians should: We are body-souls; and any discussion that considers exercise, for example, should remember that fact. David Mathis has offered a highly useful book that highlights the importance of exercise, but he does not forget that we are made in the image of God, created for his service, and most useful as we give our whole person to the Lord's work."

**Mark Jones**, Senior Minister, Faith Reformed Presbyterian Church, Vancouver, British Columbia

"The importance of regular exercise is an oft-overlooked topic in the Christian community. In *A Little Theology of Exercise*, David Mathis provides a theologically rich yet accessible look at how bodily stewardship serves our joy in God. This brief and inviting book will benefit those who already enjoy regular exercise as well as those who need a little motivation to get moving. I look forward to giving it to the men and women who take my fitness classes!"

**Sharonda Cooper**, Bible teacher; elite fitness instructor

"David Mathis has written this wonderfully helpful book about the vital role of using our bodies in our enjoyment of God. I loved reading his biblically grounded thinking that insightfully shows that the body is a marvelous gift from God but, like all his gifts, is a means to the much greater end of glorifying God through delighting in him. This book will make you want to go for a run and worship God as you do."

**K. Erik Thoennes**, Professor of Theology, Talbot School of Theology, Biola University; Pastor, Grace Evangelical Free Church, La Mirada, California

"Mathis opens *A Little Theology of Exercise* with 1 Corinthians 6:19–20: 'You are not your own, for you were bought with a price. So glorify God in your body.' He then dives deep into this truth, clarifying what our culture has obscured. God amazingly designed our bodies not for self-worship but for his glory—not to remain sedentary but to be vigorously used in service to him. Mathis urges us to be wise stewards of our bodies by staying fit, which enables us to serve God more fervently, find greater delight in him, and glorify him through our bodies. Read this book! Its rich theology will transform your perspective on exercising and help you find joy in offering your body as a living sacrifice to God."

**Bobby Scott**, Pastor of Discipleship, Community of Faith Bible Church, South Gate, California; Council Member, The Gospel Coalition; former track and field all-American

"At the core of every Christian's perspective on physical health and fitness is a motive that either seeks transformation or opts for the status quo. In this important book, David Mathis makes the biblical and gospel-centered case for joyfully pursuing a fit and balanced life for its physical, mental, and spiritual benefits—for the glory of God. In a Christian culture that rightly rejects the extremes of a sedentary or idolatrous life, we find in this Scripture-saturated work a joyful rationale for doing hard things as a means to meeting the needs of others, enjoying God more deeply, and experiencing the joy God has on offer."

**David Bush**, Founder, Fit for the King; author, *The Body Gospel* and *Fit for the King: Your Health and God's Purpose for Your Life*

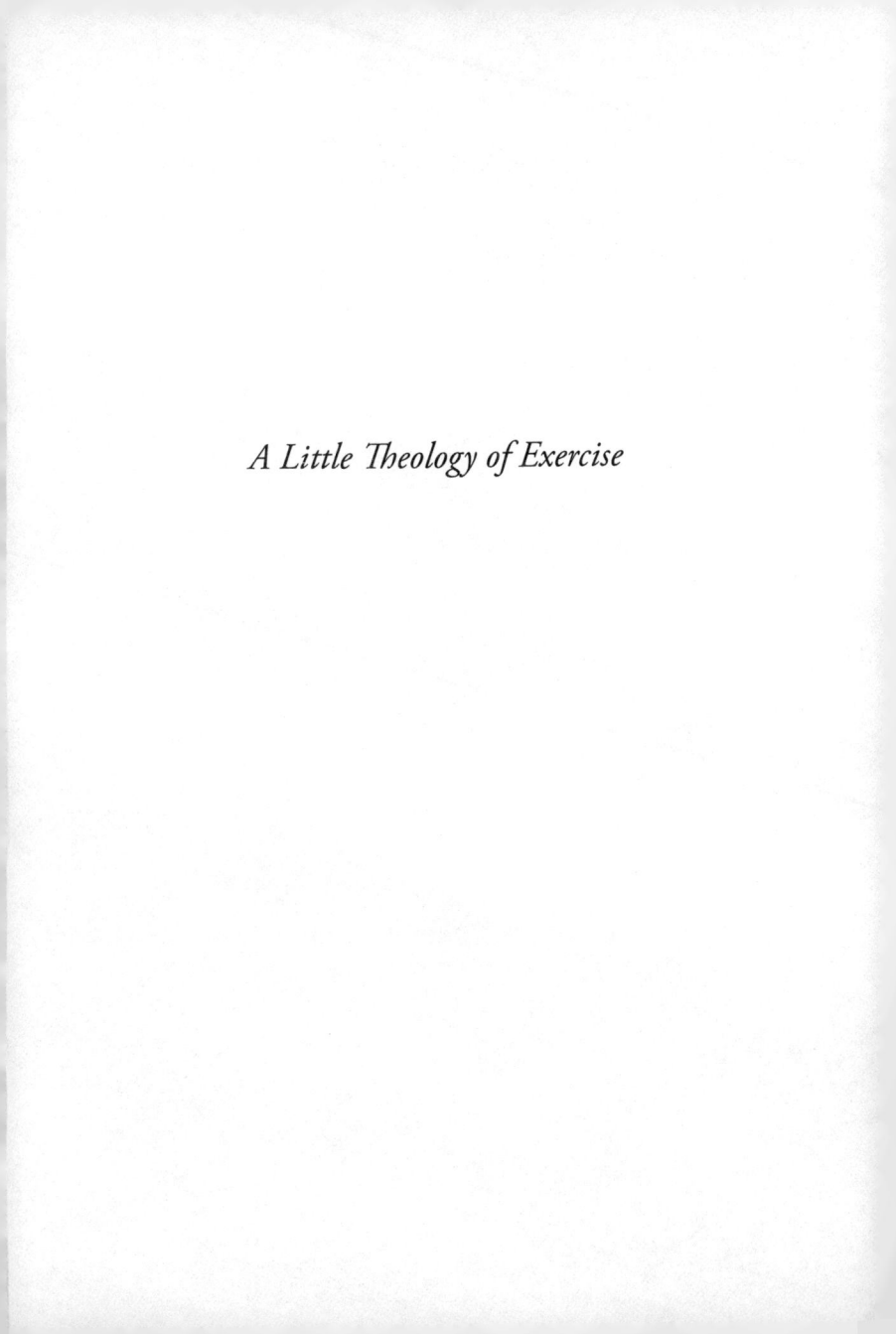

*A Little Theology of Exercise*

# A Little
# Theology of Exercise

*Enjoying Christ in Body and Soul*

David Mathis

**:: CROSSWAY®**

WHEATON, ILLINOIS

*A Little Theology of Exercise: Enjoying Christ in Body and Soul*

© 2025 by David Mathis

Published by Crossway
    1300 Crescent Street
    Wheaton, Illinois 60187

All rights reserved. No part of this publication may be reproduced, stored in a retrieval system, or transmitted in any form by any means, electronic, mechanical, photocopy, recording, or otherwise, without the prior permission of the publisher, except as provided for by USA copyright law. Crossway® is a registered trademark in the United States of America.

Cover design: David Fassett

Cover image: Getty Images, Rawpixel, Discobolus statue from Statens Museum for Kunst

First printing 2025

Printed in the United States of America

Unless otherwise indicated, Scripture quotations are from the ESV® Bible (The Holy Bible, English Standard Version®), © 2001 by Crossway, a publishing ministry of Good News Publishers. Used by permission. All rights reserved. The ESV text may not be quoted in any publication made available to the public by a Creative Commons license. The ESV may not be translated in whole or in part into any other language.

Scripture quotations marked NASB are taken from the New American Standard Bible®, copyright © 1960, 1971, 1977, 1995, 2020 by The Lockman Foundation. Used by permission. All rights reserved. www.lockman.org.

All emphases in Scripture quotations have been added by the author.

Trade paperback ISBN: 978-1-4335-9867-8
ePub ISBN: 978-1-4335-9869-2
PDF ISBN: 978-1-4335-9868-5

---

**Library of Congress Cataloging-in-Publication Data**

Names: Mathis, David, 1980- author.
Title: A little theology of exercise : enjoying Christ in body and soul / David Mathis.
Description: Wheaton, Illinois : Crossway, [2025] | Includes bibliographical references and index.
Identifiers: LCCN 2024038804 (print) | LCCN 2024038805 (ebook) | ISBN 9781433598678 (trade paperback) | ISBN 9781433598685 (pdf) | ISBN 9781433598692 (epub)
Subjects: LCSH: Theological anthropology—Christianity. | Exercise—Religious aspects—Christianity. | Soul—Christianity.
Classification: LCC BT701.3 .M359 2025 (print) | LCC BT701.3 (ebook) | DDC 261.5/61—dc23/eng/20250108
LC record available at https://lccn.loc.gov/2024038804
LC ebook record available at https://lccn.loc.gov/2024038805

---

Crossway is a publishing ministry of Good News Publishers.

| BP | | 34 | 33 | 32 | 31 | 30 | 29 | 28 | 27 | 26 | 25 |
|----|----|----|----|----|----|----|----|----|----|----|----|
| 15 | 14 | 13 | 12 | 11 | 10 | 9 | 8 | 7 | 6 | 5 | 4 | 3 | 2 | 1 |

*To John and Jon*
*Founders,*
*Desiring God*

*You are not your own,
for you were bought with a price.
So glorify God in your body.*

1 CORINTHIANS 6:19–20

# Contents

Preface *ix*

Introduction *1*
*Joy Set Before Us*

PART 1: MOVE THE BODY *15*
*Making Exercise Christian*

1 His Word *19*
 *What God Says About Our Bodies*

2 Our Prayers *39*
 *How We Ask for Help*

PART 2: CONDITION THE SOUL *45*
*Why We Exercise*

3 For Our God *51*
 *Glorify Him in the Body*

4 For the Mind *57*
 *Build and Condition the Brain*

5  For the Will   *67*
   *Learn to Lean into the Hill*

6  For Joy   *77*
   *Seek Satisfaction in Jesus*

7  For Love's Sake   *83*
   *Get Fit for Good Works*

   Conclusion   *93*
   *Move the Needle*

   Acknowledgments   *97*
   General Index   *101*
   Scripture Index   *106*
   Desiring God Note on Resources   *109*

# Preface

"MAN HAS HELD THREE VIEWS OF HIS BODY," writes C. S. Lewis in his 1960 book *The Four Loves*.

> First there is that of those ascetic Pagans who called it the prison or the "tomb" of the soul, and [others] to whom it was a "sack of dung," food for worms, filthy, shameful, a source of nothing but temptation to bad men and humiliation to good ones. Then there are the Neo-Pagans . . . , the nudists and the sufferers from Dark Gods, to whom the body is glorious. But thirdly we have the view which St. Francis expressed by calling his body "Brother Ass."[1]

Lewis then comments, "All three may be . . . defensible; but give me St. Francis for my money." He continues, "*Ass*

---

1 C. S. Lewis, *The Four Loves* (1960; repr., Harcourt Brace, 1988), 100–101.

is exquisitely right because no one in his senses can either revere or hate a donkey. It is a useful, sturdy, lazy, obstinate, patient, lovable and infuriating beast; deserving now a stick and now a carrot; both pathetically and absurdly beautiful. So the body."[2]

Just as Lewis saw these three enduring views of the human body in his day, so too we see them today. We have our ascetic (or digital) pagans, who find their physical body a prison that holds them back. But now screens and virtual reality create new possibilities. Life, for many, in the tech age has become shockingly sedentary, planted endlessly in front of screens and living increasingly through their devices.

Meanwhile, those same screens display image after image of meticulously sculpted and enhanced human bodies—these are Lewis's neo-pagans (half-nudists, at least) for whom the body is glorious or *must be glorious*, no matter the cost, however much dieting and exercise and surgery it requires.

Yet third, we have perhaps the road least traveled: Saint Francis's road. Lewis's road. And the road I aim to travel in this book. We might even call this the road of Christian Hedonists—*Christian* Hedonists. Today's non-Christian hedonists may divide themselves up, more or less, between sedentary,

---

[2] Lewis, *The Four Loves*, 101.

digital paganism and semi-exhibitionist neo-paganism, while we *Christian* Hedonists are gladly left with "Brother Ass."

I recognize the word *ass* is arresting. It accents our natural, sinful laziness and obstinance—the "infuriating beast" deserving the stick, as Lewis says. But let's not miss the affection and warmth in the word *brother*. Lewis does not say "brother" lightly. Just as Jesus doesn't say "brother" lightly. And I don't repeat "brother" lightly. *Brother* accents the usefulness, sturdiness, patience, and lovability of these bodies that are "absurdly beautiful." And even here, in recognizing their beauty, Lewis steers a careful course between genuine appreciation and holy reverence—our bodies are not to be worshiped but acknowledged and enjoyed as, in the words of the psalmist, "fearfully and wonderfully made" (Ps. 139:14).

## We Christian Hedonists

I am a pastor and Christian teacher. I am not a personal trainer. I am not a dietician. In fact, I have hardly anything to say in this book about diet—except a general plug for moderation and a broad warning about drinking sugar. But as a Christian Hedonist—as one persuaded that *God is most glorified in us when are most satisfied in him*—I have a serious interest in how the human body serves not only natural joy but also spiritual joy. And I hope, as a Christian Hedonist, that the approach of this book will land on the reader far more like a carrot than a stick.[3]

Question 1 of the Heidelberg Catechism (1563) asks, "What is your only comfort in life and in death?" The answer is this: "That I am not my own, but belong—*body and soul, in life and in death*—to my faithful Savior, Jesus Christ."[4] Much could be said about how the life of the soul affects the life of the body, and this will be implicit at some places in the following study. But in this short book, I'd like to focus on *stewarding the body*—and in particular moving the body, exercising and exerting the body, even training and conditioning the body—in service of the soul (our joy), for the praise of God (his glory), and for the good of others (love).

My hope is that this book will be useful to a wide swath of Christians—not just those already convinced of the opportunity physical exercise can be to serve spiritual life. My prayer is that Christians who are living largely sedentary lives, who are ready to consider some new habits, and who want to harness the possibilities in bodily exertion to assist their

---

[3] For more on "Christian Hedonism," see John Piper, *Desiring God: Meditations of a Christian Hedonist*, rev. ed. (Crossway, 2025), or in summary form, John Piper, *The Dangerous Duty of Delight: The Glorified God and the Satisfied Soul* (Multnomah, 2001), or visit desiringGod.org.

[4] "The Heidelberg Catechism," in *Creeds, Confessions, and Catechisms: A Reader's Edition*, ed. Chad Van Dixhoorn (Crossway, 2022), 291 (emphasis added).

joy in God will find this short study accessible and inspiring. I hope it will help you, in the context of our sedentary age, to realize and leverage the potential of your body in the service of Christian joy. I want you to freshly appreciate the gift and wonder of our bodies, designed by God for movement and exertion, as aids in our call to glorify him and as assistants (rather than obstacles) to life-transforming joy in Christ and acts of love toward others.

I also hope that Christians who are already active in physical fitness but often tempted by shallow and sinful motivations will find here the (little) theology to undergird, inform, and shape their bodily training. I pray that those who are already dedicated to exercise but driven by worldly and selfish reasons would find solid, reinforcing biblical reasons to modestly train their bodies in service to their calling as Christians to be happy in God and glorify him in their bodies.

*David Mathis*
SAINT PAUL, MINNESOTA

Introduction

# Joy Set Before Us

WHY WOULD A PASTOR, of all people, write a book about exercise?

In short, I want to help people know and enjoy Jesus more and, so, make much of him in the world as he deserves. As a pastor, that often means that I'm speaking and writing about Jesus himself,[1] or teaching portions of the Bible, or commending various *spiritual* disciplines (which I call "habits of grace"[2]). And God made us embodied creatures. The *physical* body has a vital part to play in our spiritual and holistic health and God-honoring joy. In my adult life, especially in

---

1 For instance, David Mathis, *Rich Wounds: The Countless Treasures of the Life, Death, and Triumph of Jesus* (Good Book, 2022).
2 David Mathis, *Habits of Grace: Enjoying Jesus Through the Spiritual Disciplines* (Crossway, 2016).

the last decade, I've found that *physical exercise serves my soul*, and I'm eager to commend that to you to serve your growth "in the grace and knowledge of our Lord and Savior Jesus Christ" (2 Pet. 3:18).

To be clear, my appreciation for exercise and "bodily training" (1 Tim. 4:8) is not as an end in itself. One of the reasons I take exercise seriously, rather than neglecting it, is precisely because of how it serves the joy, strength, and stability of my soul.

The issue of deliberate physical exercise, in service of the Christian life, may be more pressing in our times than for saints of old who lived in far less sedentary societies. The industrial revolution, modern travel and labor-saving technologies, and (in particular) the invention of the television—all alongside the modern diet—have brought significant changes in recent generations. In my own lifetime, the advent of the personal computer in the 1980s, the internet in the 1990s, and the smartphone in 2007 has left many of us still coming to grips with how sedentary human life can be if we are conformed to the pattern of our world. But this has not always been so. God made us to move and to do so vigorously. And he wired our brains to leverage vigorous movement, reward it, and reinforce it. Exercise makes happier humans, and God made humans to be happy—in him—with bodily movement being an assistant, rather than an adversary, to Christ-exalting joy.

## Embracing Our Humanity

Even those of us with fulltime jobs and small children typically have enough time for the real nonnegotiables of life: daily Bible meditation and prayer, weekly corporate worship, midweek Christian fellowship, generous family time, reasonable work hours, adequate sleep, *and modest exercise*.

I had a regular pattern of exercise through much of my twenties but let my habits lapse after getting married and having twin boys three years later. In the summer of 2015, I got serious about exercise again. It had been about seven years of general sedentariness. Strenuous physical activity had become far more the exception than the rule. On a June evening, while walking with my wife, I complained about not having enough time to exercise. She didn't buy it. It was a matter of my priorities, she said. I had enough time in the morning for both Bible and exercise before the kids were up. And besides, I had no business filling my schedule with so many commitments if basic human needs like sleep and exercise were continually delinquent.

So I finally owned up to the fact that if I was not getting some minimal regular exercise, I must be making some bad choices and trying to do too many things, or I must be investing my time unwisely. In a new way, I was coming to grips with my humanity. For me, making exercise a priority has had a lot to do with embracing my finitude and making time for the basics of both being a Christian (through personal and corporate habits of grace) and being human, including adequate sleep and moderate exercise.

## Wonder of Movement

In the 2009 bestseller *Born to Run*, journalist Christopher McDougall marvels at the human anatomy and physiology and at our ability for endurance running.[3] But humans are not just born to run. While animals tend to excel at one or two main abilities, God built humans for countless capacities, with the ability to adapt, specialize, and excel in many ways.

According to Harvard psychiatrist John Ratey, humans are "the Swiss Army knives of motion":

> The research on this shows no favoritism, no sweet spot according to any one activity, no real specialization, and this result is counter to what's found with any other species. For other species, one can make a categorical statement like "born to gallop," but for humans, no. Born to run?

[3] Christopher McDougall, *Born to Run: A Hidden Tribe, Superathletes, and the Greatest Race the World Has Never Seen* (Knopf, 2009).

Yes indeed, but also born for doing other activities as well. Humans are the Swiss Army knives of motion.[4]

In what other species do you see a variety that stretches from linebackers to ballerinas? Average humans like me tend to think of professional athletes and dancers as flukes of nature, born with something the rest of us were not. As we sit in front of the television or in a stadium or theater seat, it sure seems in that moment like we could never do what they're doing. *I could never move my body like that. I never could have been nearly that strong or fast.*

But what if we pause for a minute and think about how different our lives have been for the last twenty years, compared to these professionals? Or thirty years. Or forty. We were born far more alike than we tend to think. These masters of movement who capture our attention were not born with the ability to do gymnastics, or jump high into the air and land on ice skates, or hit a hundred-mile-per-hour fastball.

---

[4] John Ratey, *Go Wild: Free Your Body and Mind from the Afflictions of Civilization* (Little and Brown, 2014), 26. Elsewhere, he adds, "The human body is unique among the bodies of our close relatives, our fellow mammals, in not having a sweet spot, in having muscles and a supporting skeletal system designed for a whole variety of movements." Ratey, 121.

Rather, the human body in its divine design is capable of developing remarkable skills through practice and conditioning. However much we tend to overestimate what our bodies can do in the short run, we typically underestimate what they can do in the long run. Of course, what so markedly sets us apart from the animal kingdom, even according to evolutionary biologists, is the human brain. There is nothing else in our gloriously created world that comes close to being as advanced, complex, and astounding as the human brain.

I mention the brain in particular because of the part it plays in the wonder of human movement. The size, complexity, and power of the human brain correlate with our ability to move like no other creature. It can be amazing to watch humans move. As Ratey observes, "Sedentary as we may be, we still pay enormous amounts of money and invest enormous amounts of cultural capital in watching people move, obviously so with sports but consider, too, movement like ballet. What other species could accomplish this level of variation and control in pure movement?"[5]

## Beautiful Feet and Hands

When's the last time you paused to ponder the wonder of feet? Not just their oddness and elegance but the fact that we

---

5  Ratey, *Go Wild*, 101.

have them at all. Unlike plants and trees, we are not tethered in place by roots. We are not left to wait for the world to come to us. Rather, we can go into the world—indeed, Jesus commissioned us to do so (Matt. 28:19–20)—to step, walk, run, dance, and move. According to McDougall, "Leonardo da Vinci considered the human foot, with its fantastic weight-suspension system comprising one quarter of all the bones in the human body, 'a masterpiece of engineering and a work of art.'"[6]

Irish physical therapist Gerard Hartmann, who works with some of the world's finest distance runners, says,

> Blueprint your feet, and you'll find a marvel that engineers have been trying to match for centuries. Your foot's centerpiece is the arch, the greatest weight-bearing design ever created. The beauty of any arch is the way it gets stronger under stress; the harder you push down, the tighter its parts mesh. . . . Buttressing the foot's arch from all sides is a high-tensile web of twenty-six bones, thirty-three joints, twelve rubbery tendons, and eighteen muscles, all stretching and flexing like an earthquake-resistant suspension bridge.[7]

[6] McDougall, *Born to Run*, 156.
[7] Quoted in McDougall, *Born to Run*, 176–77.

What about the wonder of your human hands? Isaac Newton supposedly said, "In the absence of any other proof, the thumb alone would convince me of God's existence."[8] Not only do we move about the world on our feet and legs but also reach, extend, grasp, and touch with our arms and hands. We use them to work, lift, tear, cut, build, push, and pull.

No material entity in God's created world is more complex, fascinating, marvelous, and valuable than human life, which God designed to specially reflect him in his world. The reason your body and brain are so marvelous, so fearfully and wonderfully made, is to point to God—even as, in this fallen world, "our outer self is wasting away" (2 Cor. 4:16). One day, sin and death will be no more, and we will have a glorified resurrection body. Then we will experience, beyond imagination, the full, unhindered wonder of feet and hands and movement to the glory of God.

### Sedentary Times

Alongside breathing, eating, thinking, feeling, and speaking, one of the great fundamentals of human life is movement. Bodily activity is so basic, so obvious, often so assumed,

---

8 The quotation is often attributed to Newton, but I am unable to identify its source.

that we easily overlook what a veritable superpower it is. Yet movement is one vital aspect of our enduring human nature that our present age threatens to undermine.

Few today would disagree that we are living in a sedentary age compared to generations and centuries before us. One great downside of the exponential burst of modern technologies is that our bodies and their movement seem to matter less and less. As a fellow pastor insightfully observes, "Much of what we call 'technology' does not actually help us to become more productive at our work but rather does our work for us. While claiming to help us become more efficient, this sort of technology actually trains us to do little or nothing at all."[9]

We have cars, and we walk far less. We have machines and other labor-saving devices, and so we use our hands less. We have screens, and we move less. Added to that, in our prosperity and decadence, food and (sugar-saturated) drinks are available to us like never before.[10]

---

[9] Steven Wedgeworth, "Your Family Is the Frontlines: Three Ways to Recover the Christian Home," Desiring God, April 22, 2020, https://www.desiringgod.org/.

[10] According to the National Institute of Diabetes and Digestive and Kidney Diseases, now more than 40 percent of US adults are considered obese. For a short treatment of sugar (honey) from a biblical standpoint, see David Mathis, "What Is Sweeter Than Honey? A Little Theology of Sugar," Desiring God, March 22, 2021, https://www.desiringgod.org/.

INTRODUCTION

Unless we break the cycle, we will consume more, move our bodies less, and then find it ever harder to lift our own weight off the couch when some physical opportunity or request beckons. Simply walking upstairs becomes a mental barrier. Taking out the trash feels like more than a chore. Doing work around the house seems daunting.

We still *move*, of course—we must. But many of us have been conditioned by this present age and our own lazy impulses to *move as little as possible*. Now, economy of bodily movement has long been a survival instinct, in God's good design, to protect against starvation, but few reading this book are under any near threat of starvation today. Our need is not for conserving calories but for putting to good use the abundance of calories we consume (almost) without thinking.

To the degree that our default is to move as little as possible—rather than to move freely, eagerly, and enjoyably—we undermine or inhibit some essential dynamics in the Christian life. As Christians, we cannot content ourselves with taking our bearings from our sedentary society. Our modern excesses are not just of human concern but Christian concern.

## Bodies in Motion in the Bible

Regular human movement has been assumed throughout history. For instance, consider what we gather about the normalcy of bodily movement and activity from the Old and New Testaments. In one sense, we might simply observe, "They had no planes, trains, and automobiles." Adam and Eve walked out of the garden when they sinned and spent the rest of their lives working the ground with their own hands and whatever tools they were able to produce. Noah and his sons built an ark as big as a football field with their own hands and sweat. Abraham, Isaac, and Jacob were nomads—that is, they moved around and walked, herding sheep for their livelihood. So, too, Joseph and his brothers walked. Pharaoh put the Israelites to hard labor. Moses, no matter how comfortable his first forty years may have been, spent his last eighty on his feet. Which brings us to the wilderness generation, when God's people *wandered*, that is, moved about the desert for forty years.

In the time of the judges, we are confronted with two clearly negative examples of obesity: Eglon (Judg. 3:17, 22) and Eli (1 Sam. 4:18). Fat food was a blessing; fat men were not. King David, on the other hand, is represented as a kind of physical specimen. He killed Goliath *in his youth*, and he manifestly was no weak man. He was a man of war—skilled and fearsome—and according to Psalm 18 was not only deadly with projectiles but also able to outrun other men with his speed, agility, and strength.

INTRODUCTION

Inactivity in Scripture spells disaster, in time, for nations and generations, as in Deuteronomy 31:20: "When I have brought them into the land flowing with milk and honey, which I swore to give to their fathers, and they have eaten and are full and grown fat, they will turn to other gods and serve them, and despise me and break my covenant" (so also Deut. 32:15; Jer. 5:28). And when such national and literal fatness led to the destruction of the holy city by a foreign army, serving as the instrument of God's covenant justice, then the people walked on their own two feet some seven hundred miles around the desert to Babylon. And seventy years later, when Cyrus the Persian issued his decree that the temple could be rebuilt, that may have sounded like great news for believing exiles, but only a fraction of them actually took up the seven-hundred-mile journey to move back home.

### In the Body, for the Soul

Fast forward to the first century and consider how much Jesus walked. It's over one hundred miles from Capernaum on the Sea of Galilee to Jerusalem. That's not a long trip in a car or bus. But on foot? It makes for five to ten travel days—that is, walking all or most of the day. Then ponder the missionary journeys of the apostle Paul!

All this to say, one of the major differences between our times and biblical times, very practically, relates to our technologies. One of the main manifestations of that is the general sedentariness of our lives compared to theirs. And if the above summary of biblical bodily exertion makes you tired just thinking about it, consider how the orientation of our modern age on physical activity, compared to the preindustrial world, affects how we think about *doing good* for others—because doing good typically requires bodily exertion in some form. Good comes into being through working, not wishing. And apart from that, the sedentariness of our bodies is not disconnected but deeply integrated with our inner person—with our minds, hearts, and wills.

This may be one of the most surprising aspects of this study. This book is not only (or mainly) about the body but also the soul. Our bodies and souls are profoundly and mysteriously connected. What we do with one can deeply affect the other. We train our souls through conditioning our bodies, and what we do with our souls can greatly affect our bodies. This is why, as a pastor, I've written this book *on exercise* for Christians: because what we do (and don't do) with our bodies does affect our faith, our minds, our joys (with the whole range of our emotions), and our wills (whether we're willing and eager to exert our bodies to do others good).

INTRODUCTION

Countless unbelievers come to experience and enjoy the many benefits of exercise but do not adore Jesus or have the Holy Spirit. My concern is *how a Christian might exercise differently than an unbeliever.* How do we experience God's natural gift of physical exercise in such a way that we profit spiritually?

More to the point, how does the joy of exercise serve joy in God? The answer begins with theology and becomes very practical in our motivations and approach to working out. My burden is to persuade Christians of the joy and value of modest bodily training and to encourage them not merely to *factor in God* to our exercise but to *put him at the center.*

Another way to put it would be to ask, *How do I make exercise holy?* To that we turn in part 1.

## PART 1

---

# MOVE THE BODY

*Making Exercise Christian*

How do I make exercise holy?

We could approach this little theology of exercise from many angles. We could simply begin with what the Christian Scriptures teach about our bodies and then seek to make our own personal applications in that light. Or another angle is to ask the personal questions, How do I make my exercise holy? How do I make it count for God? For eternity? For what matters most? How do I exercise with God, not self, at the center?

For me, and I hope for you too, it's not enough to enjoy fitness and just happen to be a Christian. So we turn first to 1 Timothy 4, where we find some important truths about our bodies. However, we will not (yet) go where you might be expecting—to 4:8 about "bodily training." Rather, here's 1 Timothy 4:1–5:

> Now the Spirit expressly says that in later times some will depart from the faith by devoting themselves to deceitful spirits and teachings of demons, through the insincerity of liars whose consciences are seared, who forbid marriage and require abstinence from foods that God created to be received with thanksgiving by those who believe and know the truth. For everything created by God is good, and nothing is to be rejected if it is received with thanksgiving, for it is made holy by the word of God and prayer.

First, mark the anti-body orientation of the false teachers Paul opposes. They are suspicious of, to the point of opposing, basic bodily pleasures that God designed. These false teachers forbid marriage (implying the marriage bed) and certain foods. Paul does not mention *physical exercise*, but clearly the full embrace of bodily existence is in view. And 4:8 is only a

## MAKING EXERCISE CHRISTIAN

breath away with its mention of "bodily training." So this is a fitting place and context to draw out some applications to exercise—that is, "voluntary physical activity undertaken for the sake of health and fitness."[1]

Paul writes in 1 Timothy 4:4–5 that "everything created by God is good, and nothing is to be rejected if it is received with thanksgiving, for it is made holy by the word of God and prayer." I'll say more in part 2 about thanksgiving, but first let's ponder how life in the body is "made holy." How is the marriage bed made holy, and how are eating and drinking made holy? Paul says, "by the word of God and prayer."

Now, what does that mean? How do God's word and prayer "make holy" various bodily acts for which God designed and made us? In chapter 1, we will focus on "God's word" for our bodies (and exercise), and in chapter 2, we will turn to prayer—and very practically how we might respond in

---

1 Daniel Lieberman, *Exercised: Why Something We Never Evolved to Do Is Healthy and Rewarding* (Pantheon, 2021), xii. Lieberman observes that "until recently only great kings and queens could enjoy taking it easy whenever they wanted. Today in a bizarre reversal of the human condition, voluntary physical activity for the sake of health—a.k.a. exercise—has become a privilege for the privileged. In addition to being surrounded by laborsaving devices, billions of people have jobs and commutes that prevent them from being physically active by requiring them to sit for most of the day." Lieberman, 47–48.

prayer to what God tells us about our bodies. Then, in part 2 (chapters 3–7), we will explore various Christian motivations and incentives for exercise.

So what does God's word say about our bodies and their exercise?

1

# His Word

*What God Says About Our Bodies*

GOD MADE US not only to *live* our lives but to *consecrate* them. That is, he does not intend that we humans float mindlessly and unconscientiously through our daily acts but that we *make them holy*, that we set them apart from the pattern and assumptions of the unbelieving world, that we live differently than those in rebellion against God. In 1 Timothy 4:5, Paul says this making holy, this sanctifying—this consecrating of normal, human, bodily life—happens *by the word of God and prayer*. What does that mean?

*The word of God* is what God says, what he has spoken, what he has breathed out in the Scriptures for us to know about our bodies. In this chapter, which is the longest in this short book, we'll look at what God says about our bodies. Our exercise and physical exertions will not be holy if we view our bodies in ways that are not true, in subtle and overt lies not in accord with what God has revealed (and our society is teeming with such halftruths).

*Prayer*, then, is our response back to God in light of what he has said. We'll turn to how we might pray for our exercise in chapter 2.

Two questions now lie before us in this chapter and the next: (1) What does God say, in his word, about our bodies? What God-designed and God-revealed truths *about our bodies* inform the Christian life and our movement and exercise? And (2) how do we make bodily exertions and training holy through prayer by speaking back to God in light of what he has revealed?

So, what does God say about our bodies?

### His Story, Our Bodies

For those in Christ, we learn to view our bodies in layers—layers of a redemptive story. Our bodies are not only fearfully and wonderfully complex but also vitally *en-storied*. Understanding our past (as human), our future (in glory), and our present (in the Spirit) is critical for duly appreciating, chastening, and leveraging our bodies for Jesus in this life. Let's rehearse the story in six acts.

## WHAT GOD SAYS ABOUT OUR BODIES

### *1. God Made Our Bodies*

*First, God designed them.* The human body is fearfully and wonderfully made—both in general and in the particular body he made for you.

> You formed[1] my inward parts;
>   you knitted me together in my mother's womb.
> I praise you, for I am fearfully and wonderfully made.
>   (Ps. 139:13–14)

This is not just a pro-life text. It is that and more. It includes God's stunning design, making, and shaping of our human bodies inside and outside the womb. Brother or sister in Christ, you are "fearfully and wonderfully made." *Made.*

---

[1] For some readers, the word "formed" may bring to mind Gen. 2:7 and 2:22 (though different Hebrew words are used), which explain how God formed Adam first and then Eve, something to which Paul calls attention in 1 Tim. 2:12–13. God formed them both human but did not make them the same—he designed and built two kinds of humans, male and female. Even in an age losing its bearings about men and women, many in the fitness community today know this well and can appreciate that men and women are fearfully and wonderfully both human and different. I will not have space to address the complementary differences between men and women (which are not irrelevant to exercise), but for a brief study on the complementarity of men and women made in God's image, see John Piper, *What's the Difference: Manhood and Womanhood Defined According to the Bible* (Crossway, 2008).

Built. Designed. Your human body, your human brain, your human eyes, all bear the unmistakable marks of the universe's master builder, master craftsman, and master designer, who is God himself. You are not the product of impersonal forces, such as time, chance, and natural selection. You are designed. Spectacularly built. Fearfully and wonderfully made—both in the past as you were in the womb and at present as you read this book.

The apostle Paul says in Romans 1:20 that God's "invisible attributes, namely, his eternal power and divine nature, have been clearly perceived, ever since the creation of the world." Psalm 19:1 says that "the heavens declare the glory of God." And not only is the glory of our Creator revealed in the creation around us—the skies, the seas, the mountains, the plains, and all the animal kingdom—but we ourselves, we creatures, also proclaim his glory. Right under our noses—in fact, our very eyes, ears, and noses—are even far more striking evidences of the brilliance and skill and wisdom of our designer and maker who is God himself.

*Second, our bodies belong to God.* Contrary to the voices we hear at every turn today, *your body is not your own.* "Do you not know that your body is a temple of the Holy Spirit within you, whom you have from God? You are not your own, for you were bought with a price" (1 Cor. 6:19–20). *Your body is not your own.* It belongs to God. He made it and owns it. This is doubly true for Christians because God both created us and then redeemed us at the infinite cost of his own Son.

*Third, our bodies are for God.* Our bodies are for use in the service and honor of their Creator, which means, ultimately, that our bodies are for God's glory. This can sound strange to modern ears. Perhaps especially in the fitness community. "My body is for the purpose of my glory" is likely not said aloud. But how often, even among Christians, is this the operative principle?

But when we open Scripture and hear what God says, when we seek to make our bodily activity and training holy by his word, by what he says about our bodies, we see that our bodies—indeed all our lives—are for his glory. We exist to glorify God. God made us to enjoy him and make him look good. That's the last part of 1 Corinthians 6:19–20: "You are not your own, for you were bought with a price. So glorify God in your body."

Not: Escape your body to glorify him. But: Glorify God *in your body*. Your body is meant for glorifying God, not self. For making God look good, not self look good. You exist for God's glory, and you have a body—however able or disabled—for his glory. So Paul says, "Whether you eat or drink, or whatever you do, do all to the glory of God" (1 Cor. 10:31). And in

Colossians 3:17, he makes our calling explicitly Christian, specifically about Jesus, saying, "Whatever you do, in word or deed, do everything in the name of the Lord Jesus, giving thanks to God the Father through him."

As a Christian, you have a body for Jesus's sake. As a Christian, his name is on you. In coming to Christ and receiving baptism, we have taken his name on ourselves. We are called *Christians*. His name has been put on us publicly, and what we do with our minds, hearts, mouths, *and bodies*—either directly or indirectly—makes Jesus look good or is in vain.

God made our bodies. He designed and owns them; they are for him. And he is for them: "The body is . . . for the Lord, and the Lord for the body" (1 Cor. 6:13). But what he has to say about our bodies does not end there.

## 2. Sin Has Seized Our Bodies

Next comes the tragic and grievous truth that we—and our bodies with us—are fallen.

Sin wracks our bodies not only in the effects of the curse into which we're born but also in our own desiring and doing of evil. The bodies God gave us to image him as we move about his created world have become bodies of sin and death (Rom. 6:6; 7:24; 8:10). No longer the original unfallen creations (nor yet the coming imperishable bodies), they are now mortal bodies (Rom. 6:12; 8:11), dishonored in our sin (Rom. 1:24). We will be judged for what we do in the body (2 Cor. 5:10). And apart from God's redemptive provision, we will be thrown—soul *and body*—into hell (Matt. 5:29, 30; 10:28).

Our forefather Adam sinned against God's command—his one *no* in a world of *yes*. And God, in response to human rebellion, and as an ongoing reminder of it, cursed the creation, including our bodies.

> The creation was subjected to futility, not willingly, but because of him [God] who subjected it, in hope that the creation itself will be set free from its bondage to corruption and obtain the freedom of the glory of the children of God. For we know that the whole creation has been groaning together in the pains of childbirth until now. And not only the creation, but we ourselves, who have the firstfruits of the Spirit, groan inwardly as we wait eagerly for adoption as sons, the redemption of our bodies. (Rom. 8:20–23)

Not only does our fallen world groan, but so do *we ourselves!* Because of human sin, this world and our bodies strain under the power and effects of sin. They are not what they once were.

They break down. They become diseased and get injured—sometimes oh so easily.

However, even though marred by sin, they still remain a marvel. It is all too easy for those of us who are still relatively physically fit and enjoy some measure of good health to fail to marvel that we can stand and move, keep our balance, lift heavy objects, walk for half an hour, or even run several miles.

In this fallen and cursed creation, many great saints are terminally kept from the pleasures of God in exercise. Disabilities abound in the present age. And God has his particular manifestations of mercy for the disabled and their caregivers. Disability can be a great tragedy and great burden to bear. Those of us who are able to move and exercise our bodies would do well to be more regularly and consciously thankful to God. An able body in this sin-sick world is a precious gift not to be taken for granted.

### A Word on Disability

For those in Christ living with disabilities, God's grace is sufficient for our thorns (2 Cor. 12:9), and he has his alternate ways of communicating natural and spiritual pleasures to inhibited saints. One dear brother I know more than makes up for every mile he doesn't run with a monstrous belly laugh, the kind of laugh known only to those who have suffered greatly and found God stronger than every pain. Whether your body is young and vigorous—or old, injured, or disabled—1 Corinthians 6:20 speaks to you too: "Glorify God in your body."

However old, sick, or diseased your body may be, God has given it to you as your particular vessel to glorify him—the God who turns the world upside down in the seeming weakness and folly of the cross (1 Cor. 1:18–29). My aim in this book is to think Christianly, not naturally or carnally, about bodily health and physical ability. As we will see, there is a real, discernable boost for the spirit in physical exercise. I think that those who are able are wise to leverage it.

But for those unable to exercise, hope is not lost. It's just a boost. God made our human souls to be "boosted" by bodily activity and exertion but not dependent on it. Disability is not devastating to genuine joy. You can be profoundly happy in Jesus without this boost. Many of the world's happiest Christians are precisely that. God has his ways for making up for this physical loss in saints who are unable to exert and exercise their bodies.

### 3. *God Himself Took a Human Body*

In our fallen world, God's redemptive provision, stunning in so many ways, begins with the incarnation when God himself took a fully human body in the person of his eternal Son. And he not only took on our human flesh and blood but also gave up his body to death on a cross to cover our sin and rescue us (Phil. 2:8).

If you come to the Christian Scriptures with questions about your own physical body, one of the first surprises may be how much the New Testament talks about the physical body of Jesus (Rom. 7:4; 1 Cor. 10:16; 11:24, 27, 29). His human body is the turning point in the story of our bodies. Jesus "bore our sins *in his body* on the tree" (1 Pet. 2:24). Hebrews memorably puts Psalm 40 on the lips of Jesus when he came into the world as man: "A body have you prepared for me. . . . Behold, I have come to do your will, O God" (Heb. 10:5, 7, quoting Ps. 40:6–8). The author of Hebrews then comments, "By that will we have been sanctified through the offering of the body of Jesus Christ once for all" (Heb. 10:10).

Because sin, its curse, and death have infected us in both soul and body, the divine Son took on both a human soul and body; and he gave his body up in sacrificial death to rescue us, soul and body, who are joined to him by faith.

## 4. *God Himself Dwells in Our Bodies*

Perhaps the part of the body's story most often overlooked is that God himself not only became human in Christ but also now dwells in his people by his Holy Spirit. When 1 Corinthians 6:19 says, "Your body is a temple of the Holy Spirit within you, whom you have from God," the emphasis is not on how impressive our bodies are *as temples*. Rather, the focus is the spectacular reality that God himself in his *Holy Spirit* has taken up residence, as it were, "within you"—you *have* the Spirit. Your body is a temple *because you have him*. This is almost too good to be true. It is news to receive with the kind of pulsating joy that comes "with fear and trembling" (Phil. 2:12)—God himself is in you and at work in you.

Paul makes it plain. If you are in Christ,

> the Spirit of God *dwells in you*. . . . [And] if *Christ is in you*, although the body is dead because of sin, the Spirit is life because of righteousness. If the Spirit of him who raised Jesus from the dead *dwells in you*, he who raised Christ Jesus from the dead will also give life to your mortal bodies through his Spirit who *dwells in you*. (Rom. 8:9–11)

In case you missed it, if you are in Christ, "Christ is in you"—his Holy Spirit, the Spirit of Christ, "dwells in you" (as Paul repeats). You not only have indwelling sin (no. 2 above) but now also have *the indwelling Spirit.* Our human bodies have become dwelling places for God, whom we *have* in the person of his Spirit.

## 5. We Glorify God Now in Our Bodies

Now, because of Christ's bodily work outside of us and because of his Spirit's work inside of us, we live to the glory of God. So Paul says to us in Christ, "You are not your own, for you were bought with a price. So glorify God *in your body*" (1 Cor. 6:19–20).

Already our bodies of humiliation have become instruments for God's glory. And they *are being redeemed* both as we (positively) magnify God in our affections and actions of love for him and neighbor, and as we (negatively) "by the Spirit . . . put to death the deeds of the body" (Rom. 8:13).

So we pray, like Paul, that "Christ will be honored *in my body*, whether by life or by death" (Phil. 1:20). Given the depth and pervasive effects of sin in our bodies, we might think we need to get out of these bodies in order to glorify God; but because of Christ's body and the dwelling of his Spirit in our bodies, we can now honor Christ and glorify

God *in our bodies*. So, in Christ, we realize how our bodies truly are "for the Lord" (1 Cor. 6:13).

The Christian life is an embodied life. God doesn't free us from our bodies at conversion, as if they were prisons. He leaves us in them—glorious and broken as they are. The Christian life, growth, ministry, and love happen in the body. This is our tent for life in Christ in this age. And in particular, three important truths clarify the bodily existence of the Christian life.

*First, God is for the body.* God is not opposed to our bodily existence; neither is he uninterested. He is *for the body*. As we've already seen, "The body is . . . for the Lord, and *the Lord for the body*" (1 Cor. 6:13).

*Second, God commends bodily exertion.* God plainly commends the use of our bodies through the effort of work (Eph. 4:28; 2 Thess. 3:10), even hard work (2 Tim. 2:6)—that we not be idle but "busy at work" (2 Thess. 3:11). Laziness is sin and both a physical and spiritual danger (Prov. 21:25). In particular, 1 Timothy 4:8 (the verse you may have been waiting on) affirms the value of bodily training. And that affirmation comes on top of the assumption in ancient times of a far greater degree of physical activity in the course of normal life and occupation, not to mention travel. And even in that more active context in the ancient world, the apostle does not condemn but commends physical training.

*Third, spiritual health is ultimate; physical health is not.* In other words, an asymmetrical relationship exists between our eternal souls and temporal bodies. This is an important clarification, often overlooked in efforts to rescue the physical life from neglect and spiritualism. For the Christian, the charge to bodily exertion is qualified. In appropriating what God has said about our bodies and their training, it is essential that we observe the balancing word of 1 Timothy 4:8: "While bodily training is of some value, godliness is of value in every way, as it holds promise for the present life and also for the life to come." The recognition that "bodily training is of some value" cuts both ways. Those today who are sedentary by choice need to hear that God does indeed value the exertion of our bodies (and designed them to work best and happiest when moving), and those who are prone to make exercise an idol need to hear that it is only of *some* value, relativized by the pursuit of godliness, which "is of value in every way."[2]

2  I understand "godliness" to be spiritual maturity or holiness (2 Pet. 1:5–7; 3:11). Christians are to pursue godliness and train themselves for it (1 Tim. 4:7; 6:11) through Christian teaching and by faith (1 Tim. 6:3; Titus 1:1). Such godliness is perfectly embodied in Jesus, the God-man (1 Tim. 3:16). I treat "godliness" as synonymous with "Christlikeness," in both the inner and outer person.

The health of the soul being ultimate doesn't mean that the health of the body is insignificant or marginal. This is where some Christians have gone wrong. Rather, bodily movement and exertion are important, and as Christians we put the body to work in service of our souls and the souls of others.

So even now, in this life, we seek to glorify God in our bodies. Whereas we once presented our bodies to sin, we now present them to God as *living* sacrifices (Rom. 12:1). We do not sacrifice our bodies for Christ in the way he sacrificed his body for us—that is, redemptively. He *died* (and rose again) to rescue us. We *live* for him (which could lead to our dying) as those rescued by him. His sacrificial death is the cause; our sacrificial living is the effect. And to that end, we discipline our bodies (1 Cor. 9:27), refuse to let sin reign in our mortal bodies (Rom. 6:12), and so pray and repent and act that our bodies "be kept blameless" till the day of Christ (1 Thess. 5:23).

The healthy Christian life is no passive existence. The words of Jesus and his apostles call us to action again and again. As J. C. Ryle observes,

> It would not be difficult to point out at least twenty-five or thirty distinct passages in the epistles where believers are plainly taught to use active personal exertion, and are addressed as responsible for doing energetically what

Christ would have them do, and are not told to "yield themselves" up as passive agents and sit still, but to arise and work. A holy violence, a conflict, a warfare, a fight, a soldier's life, a wrestling, are spoken of as characteristic of the true Christian.[3]

## 6. We Await a Spectacular Bodily Upgrade

Our future will be forever embodied—beyond our best imagining. At that coming day of Christ, he "will transform our lowly body [literally, "the body of our humiliation"] to be like his glorious body" (Phil. 3:21).

Here we live, like Jesus did, in a state of humiliation. Even as we experience some of the original glories of our human bodies, they are short-lived. Soon enough, we age, we suffer tragedies and losses, and we realize increasingly what a state of humiliation this life is in these bodies. And if Christ does not return first, we soon will endure the great humiliation of death.

But for those in Christ, the dishonor of death will give way to the glory of resurrection. Our natural bodies will be sown in death like seeds that will spring up and blossom, through Christ's resurrection power, into bodies of glory

---

[3] J. C. Ryle, *Holiness: Its Nature, Hindrances, Difficulties and Roots* (1879; repr., Counted Faithful, 2015), location 217, Kindle.

like his own risen body. "What is sown is perishable; what is raised is imperishable. It is sown in dishonor; it is raised in glory. It is sown in weakness; it is raised in power. It is sown a natural body; it is raised a spiritual body" (1 Cor. 15:42–44).

Note well, this will be a spiritual *body*—not merely a *spirit*, like a ghost—but a *spiritual body* fit for the fullness of the Holy Spirit in the rock-solid world of the new heavens and new earth. Contrary to the bad pop theology of some, Christians have believed for two thousand years that *our future will be embodied.*

Not only is God *for the body* in this age but also in the age to come. Above we saw 1 Corinthians 6:13: "The body is . . . for the Lord, and the Lord for the body." The next verse reads, "God raised the Lord and will also raise us up by his power" (1 Cor. 6:14). The creative brilliance and glory of God's design in the human body will not be discarded at Christ's second coming. Finally we will be fully set free. Our bodies will shine out with the fullness of God's purpose. Our future is embodied. Faithful Christian theology does not diminish the importance of our bodies but heightens it—from God's creative design, to his ongoing affirmation, to his promise to raise them, to his calling to use them even now.

One day soon Jesus will transform our lowly, earthly, natural bodies to be like his glorious, heavenly, supernatural body—that is, the body he still has. He rose again bodily. He ascended bodily. He now sits at the right hand of God in heaven in his fully human, glorified body. When he comes back bodily, brings heaven with him to earth, and establishes the physical, embodied new world, we will enjoy (with him) what it means to have a fully human, glorified body.

**Praise the Man of Heaven**

If you are in Christ, your resurrection body will be spectacular. No more aches and pains. No more colds and COVID. No more sprains, contusions, and broken bones. No more heart attacks, strokes, and cancer. No more disease. No more devastating physical and mental disabilities.

Soon enough, you will shine like the sun in your perfected, strong, beautiful, imperishable, glorified human body. And the best part of all isn't what *your body* will be like but *whom* our imperishable bodies and souls will help us to know, enjoy, be near, and praise—the man of heaven. "Just as we have borne the image of the man of dust [Adam], we shall also bear the image of the man of heaven [Jesus Christ]" (1 Cor. 15:49).

The focus in the new heavens and new earth won't be on our bodies. Our perfected bodies will no longer experience the many distractions and drawbacks of our previous humiliations. They will enhance and support our making much of our King. Our focus in glory will be the one whom we eagerly await right now—the man of heaven.

2

# Our Prayers

*How We Ask for Help*

NOW THAT WE HAVE TRACED some of the riches of what God says about our bodies, what do we do about it? Remember, according to 1 Timothy 4:4–5, it is not enough only to hear what God has to say about our bodily exercise. *Making bodily life holy* involves prayer—asking God for help. We consecrate our bodies and exercise to God "by the word of God and prayer" (1 Tim. 4:5)—through what he says to us (in his word) *and* what we say back to him (in our prayers). So what do we say?

## Receive Exercise as a Gift

*First, we thank him.* "Everything created by God is good, and nothing is to be rejected if it is *received with thanksgiving*"

(1 Tim. 4:4). Step one in responding to what God revealed to us is receiving our bodies as the gifts they are—not taking physical movement and exertion for granted but explicitly thanking God. Gratitude is the very basic and appropriate response of the creature toward his Creator, fulfilling our purpose to "honor him as God" and "give thanks to him" (Rom. 1:21). And so we may pray something like this: "Father, thank you that my legs and lungs work like they do. Thank you for arms that swing and lift. Thank you for balance and that I don't have an ailment or other condition that confines me to bed."

Whatever body God has given you with its strengths and weaknesses is an occasion to thank him and to do so regularly. Just as each new meal can be a good prompt to thank him for his provision of food, so also the beginning (or end) of a workout or physical activity is an opportunity to thank him for the gift of your body and energy. It's also a chance to thank him for his grace to us in Christ. As Christians, we not only acknowledge God as our Creator but Christ as our Redeemer. We are doubly "not our own," as we saw in the previous chapter—we did not create our bodies (and souls) nor did we pay the price to redeem them. As Paul says in 1 Corinthians 6:19–20, "You are not your own, for *you were bought with a price*. So glorify God in your body."

Receiving thankfully the ability to move and exercise is a vital starting point, but there's more.

## Ask God for Help

We do more than simply thank God for what he has given us and done for us in Christ. We also turn to the future with faith—to activity ahead, the energy we will need, the life to be lived—and *ask him for help*.

To get practical, perhaps you pray this the night before exercising: "Father, please give me sleep tonight and the will to overcome laziness tomorrow morning. Help me to get out of bed, put on my workout clothes, lace up my shoes, and put one foot in front of the other—and then work such discipline throughout my life in the fight against sin."

Or maybe at the beginning of your workout you ask, "Father, give me the drive to push my body beyond comfort, to 'discipline my body and keep it under control' (1 Cor. 9:27). Work in me, by your Spirit, so that this physical training serves the ripening of the spiritual fruit of self-control (Gal. 5:23)."

For me, my typical prayer point for exercise is the beginning of the activity. My most frequent exercise is running, and I've made it a habit to pray as I'm setting out on a run: "Father, make this run holy to you this morning." I may say, "I consecrate this half hour to you. Give me energy, help me endure, keep me from injury, and use this exercise to boost my brain, joy, and body. And help me love others well today. May you be glorified in my body."

Another way you might pray regarding exercise is this: "Father, guard me from valuing bodily training more than godliness. Rather, make these efforts holy, through my acting in faith, so that this exercise serves my Christlikeness instead of competing with it."

Or: "Father, loosen my grip on my own performance, results, and personal goals. May my exercise not ultimately be about me but about my richer enjoyment of Jesus and my readiness to love and serve others."

Or: "Father, grant that I would know you and enjoy you more through pushing my body in this way. Let me feel your pleasure through this natural gift so that I am spiritually satisfied enough to sacrifice my own preferences and personal routines to meet the needs of others."

### Exercise Christian Faith

You might pray the night before. And pray as you begin a workout. And even pray at key moments during the workout—as I often do when starting up a long hill with little energy late in a run. And pray afterwards, thanking the one who designed your body, made it, and sustains it.

Exercise *as a Christian* by exercising in light of what God says about your body in his word and by praying with gratitude for his help, blessing, and smile on your bodily training. Don't exercise with the presumption of unbelievers but consecrate your workouts—make them holy—through the word of God and prayer.

PART 2

---

# CONDITION THE SOUL

*Why We Exercise*

"When I run, I feel God's pleasure."

Such were the memorable words of Olympic sprinter and future Christian missionary Eric Liddell (born in 1902), at least through the lens of *Chariots of Fire*, the 1981 Oscar-winning film that told his story.[1] However much this

---

1 *Chariots of Fire*, directed by Hugh Hudson (20th Century-Fox, 1981). For a brief summary of Liddell's life and Christian faith, see Jonathan Boyd, "Eric Liddell:

famous movie line represents him, the real Liddell clearly *enjoyed* running (and didn't just *tolerate* it). With the last half century of research in view, some of us might find it fascinating to introduce Liddell (who died in 1945) to the fairly recent discovery of endorphins (in the 1970s)—and more recently, endocannabinoids.

The word *endorphins* is a shortened form of the phrase "endogenous morphine." These morphine-like chemicals originate within our bodies. They block pain signals and can contribute to a euphoric feeling. It wasn't until as recently as 1974 that two independent groups first discovered and documented this long-undiscovered divine kindness tucked quietly inside the human brain. Endorphins and their effect of bodily pleasure subconsciously incline humans toward certain activities, like raucous laughter or spicy foods. But in particular, the most notable and discussed is *vigorous aerobic exercise*.

The hormones we know as endorphins may indeed play a part in the so-called runner's high. However, more is involved in the pleasant effects of exercise than just endorphins—including serotonin, dopamine, and oxytocin, among others.

---

Olympic Glory—and After," in *Sketches of Faith: An Introduction to Characters from Christian History*, ed. John D. Woodbridge (10Publishing, 2020), 193–95.

More recently, researchers have focused on the contribution of endocannabinoids. If endorphins are the body's own morphine, these are "the brain's own marijuana."[2] They blunt pain and have been described by neurologists as "the 'don't worry, be happy' chemicals."[3] According to Stanford lecturer Kelly McGonigal,

> Scientists have long speculated that endorphins are behind the runner's high, and studies show that high-intensity exercise causes an endorphin rush. But [University of Arizona anthropologist David] Raichlen had in mind another candidate, a class of brain chemicals called endocannabinoids . . . the same chemicals mimicked by cannabis, or marijuana. Endocannabinoids alleviate pain and boost mood. . . . And many of the effects of cannabis are consistent with descriptions of exercise-induced highs, including the sudden disappearance of worries or stress, a reduction in pain, the slowing of time, and a heightening of the senses.[4]

---

2 John Ratey, *Spark: The Revolutionary New Science of Exercise and the Brain* (Little and Brown, 2008), 277.

3 Kelly McGonigal, *The Joy of Movement: How Exercise Helps Us Find Happiness, Hope, Connection, and Courage* (Avery, 2019), 22.

4 McGonigal, *The Joy of Movement*, 16.

My experience as a very amateur runner is that you don't have to be accomplished to "feel God's pleasure" in and because of intense bodily exertion—especially when you push yourself and persist in it.[5] Pushing our bodies can do us much good and contribute to layers of joy and contentment. God made us to move and made movement to contribute to our health and happiness. And the holy pursuit of pleasure is an unblushing Christian concern throughout the pages of Scripture and most pointedly so in the words of Christ himself who speaks as often as anyone about *reward*.

Let me make clear that as I explain why I exercise, I do so unapologetically as a Christian Hedonist. I'll say more about this below. I believe that *God is most glorified in us when we are most satisfied in him.* So I want my life to center on *glory* and *joy*—God's glory in and through me, and my joy in and through him. I come to the topic of exercise unashamedly in pursuit of my joy in God. I exercise my body for the sake of my soul. I am seeking to make physical exercise serve spiritual joy in God. I want to leverage the body God gave me for my joy in him to his glory and the good of others.

---

5 For this reason, McGonigal has dubbed it *the persistence high*. She says to "do something that is moderately difficult for you and stick with it for at least twenty minutes. That's because the runner's high isn't a running high. It's a persistence high." McGonigal, *The Joy of Movement*, 18.

In other words, I want to treat bodily training as a servant, not a competitor, of Christlikeness.

---

Having reviewed what God says about our bodies and exercise, as well as how we might consecrate our exercise through prayer, we turn now in part 2 to motivation. We will look at five particular *Christian* reasons to exercise. These are unavoidably personal. In the last decade, all five have proved significant for me. They prompt me to set aside time, get out of bed, lace up my shoes, and embrace discomfort in the moment for the joy set before me.

My hope in identifying and explaining these five reasons is that you will refine, deepen, and sanctify your motivation for exercise. I offer these as invitations.

3

# For Our God

*Glorify Him in the Body*

FIRST AND FOREMOST, I exercise to glorify God in my body. One way among many that I can bring glory to God is to put my body to work—not working *for* my salvation but working *out* my salvation. It pleases him when we put to work the bodies he made in service of him. And when my muscles and lungs are in good condition, I'm better prepared to glorify him in my body—not just while exercising but in all of life.

## To Reflect God's Glory

As we celebrated in chapter 1, God made us *for his glory*. He created us "in his own image" (Gen. 1:27). We were made to reflect and display him, to be mobile monuments to God's strength and beauty, not to be stationary statues. We are living, breathing, speaking, working, moving images of God himself, going out into his created world to display his glory everywhere. He thought it best that his imagers not be fixed to the ground like trees and plants but instead have feet, legs, arms, and hands to move around, spread abroad, and fill the earth with his glory.

Without a doubt, God has his spectacular ways of glorifying himself through disability. But typically, some form of physical exertion becomes the occasion of imaging him in the world. To draw honor to him, we present our "*bodies* as a *living* sacrifice" (Rom. 12:1). Next verse: "Do not be conformed to this [sedentary?] world, but be transformed by the renewal of your mind" (Rom. 12:2)—that you might present *your body* "holy and acceptable to God" (12:1).

Like King David and Christ himself, we receive *the body* God has prepared for us as our vessel for doing his will (Ps. 40:6–8; Heb. 10:5–7). And Christ "bore our sins *in his body* on the tree, that we might die to sin and live to righteousness" (1 Pet. 2:24). The apostle Paul eagerly expected and hoped that "Christ will be honored *in my body*, whether by life or by death" (Phil. 1:20).

Glorifying God in our bodies is not mainly about what we avoid and don't do with them. It is far more about what we do with them—where we go with our feet, what we do with our hands to help others, and what we say with our mouths to give meaning to the acts of our bodies.

Consider the life of Christ, a story that presumes bodily exertion from beginning to end. He is the climactic image of the invisible God (2 Cor. 4:4; Col. 1:15), who lived perfectly to the glory of his Father (John 17:4, 6, 26). Even a cursory reading of the Gospels makes plain that he did not live anything close to the sedentary life that entraps so many today. Apart from the obvious—no cars, trains, planes, screens, phones, modern medicines, or processed foods—*Jesus walked essentially everywhere he went.* He moved and spent most of his waking time on his feet, as did most working-class humans in the ancient world. We see the same with Paul in Acts and in his letters. When traveling, a day's journey would have been twenty to twenty-five miles (essentially walking a marathon). When not traveling, he would have easily walked five miles (about ten thousand steps) or more doing daily work as a builder or tentmaker.

And Jesus didn't just move his feet but also his hands—lifting, cutting, tearing, pushing, holding, tugging. He worked construction for decades, growing up in the home of a tradesman. And though he was "a man of sorrows" (because of our sin) and "acquainted with grief" (Isa. 53:3), we get the impression again and again from the Gospels that he was deeply happy and emotionally stable—happy enough to bless others through tireless teaching and inconvenient healing, to promise rewards, to show compassion, and to control his righteous anger. At least such normal, daily actions meant his emotional health wasn't encumbered by a sedentary lifestyle.

**Whatever You Do**

Let's not pass over this too quickly: God made you for his glory. And our first calling as Christians is to glorify him, honor him, and make him look good in and through our lives. This is what it means to be made in his image (Gen. 1:27). What does an image do? It images. It reflects. It displays. It makes visible. God made us to image him, reflect him, and display him in this created world. We are meant to live in this creation as God himself would live if he were a creature in the world he made. And in fact, God himself *did* enter our world in creaturely, human form.

The second person of the eternal Godhead came as man— as Jesus of Nazareth. We are *in* the image of God. Jesus *is* the image of God (2 Cor. 4:4; Col. 1:15). He was God himself among us (John 1:14). He lived his human life in fulfillment of God's designs, perfectly glorifying him. And that's our calling as Christians. Not to be Jesus. Not to be God as man. But to increasingly live up to the calling to live *in God's image* as perfectly modeled and accomplished by Jesus. So, "whether you eat or drink, or whatever you do, do all to the glory of God" (1 Cor. 10:31).

Again, *glorifying God with our bodies is not mainly about what we don't do.* It's easy to focus on unrighteous acts from which we should abstain, but glorifying God in our bodies is first and foremost a positive pursuit and opportunity. As in the parable of the talents, our bodies are gifts from him to grow and develop, not bury and let languish.

4

# For the Mind

*Build and Condition the Brain*

ON WEEKDAYS I SPEND most of my work time in front of a screen. As a pastor who teaches, writes, and edits for a living, I am not paid to lift, dig, carry, push, or even move (other than my fingers). My job is not *physically* demanding, though it is often *emotionally* taxing enough that I'd be happy to swap in some manual labor.

Not that I want to do hard physical work full time! I enjoy mental labor—reading, researching, thinking, brainstorming, writing, and editing. Yet I've learned that I cannot undertake those sedentary tasks *at my best* when the rest of my life is sedentary. My brain is wonderfully served by bodily movement.

As I've aged, I've sensed more tangibly how much better I feel that day after exercise and more generally with a pattern of exercise in my life. In particular, I seem to think more clearly, more effortlessly, more creatively, and with more focus and mental stamina. Overall, when exercising regularly, I sense that I have more energy not only for further exertion but also for thinking and working hard with my mind. I've heard other people say the same.

But is this just in our heads, or is there any known biological basis for it? Can we get some clarity about this perceived mental clarity?

### The Point of Exercise?

A few years ago, I stumbled upon a book by a professor of psychiatry at Harvard Medical School named John Ratey. He spent most of his career focusing on ADHD and cowrote an important work in the field. As a doctor, former amateur athlete, and runner, he had noticed over the years how exercise seemed to serve as amazing "medicine" for his patients. Eventually, he put his findings together in the 2008 book *Spark: The Revolutionary New Science of Exercise and the Brain*.[1]

---

[1] John Ratey, *Spark: The Revolutionary New Science of Exercise and the Brain* (Little and Brown, 2008).

## BUILD AND CONDITION THE BRAIN

Now, if it sounds too good to be true—that exercise demonstrably improves brain function—remember what the prescription is here: *exercise*. Apparently, many people just want to take pills. Few want to take exercise. The prescription may be simple, but it's not easy.

Here's how Ratey opens the book:

> We all know that exercise makes us feel better, but most of us have no idea why. We assume it's because we're burning off stress or reducing muscle tension or boosting endorphins, and we leave it at that. But the real reason we feel so good when we get our blood pumping is that it *makes the brain function at its best*, and in my view, this benefit of physical activity is far more important—and fascinating—than what it does for the body. Building muscles and conditioning the heart and lungs are essentially side effects. I often tell my patients that *the point of exercise is to build and condition the brain*.[2]

How many of us have started some new exercise regimen because we felt overweight and out of shape or because we were confronted with metrics from a doctor? We wanted to

---

2 Ratey, *Spark*, 3 (emphasis added).

reduce our cholesterol, lower our weight, live longer, or look better. All these benefits, motivating as they may be for millions, are at best *side effects* of regular exercise.

The point of exercise, in our sedentary modern lives, is building and conditioning our brains. Ratey continues, "To keep our brains at peak performance, our bodies need to work hard. . . . The brain responds like muscles do, growing with use, withering with inactivity"—and movement activates the brain.[3] Then Ratey explains *how it is* that exercise improves learning—which matters to us as Christians seeking to love our Lord with heart, soul, strength, *and mind*.

### Exercise Improves Learning

As Christians, we call ourselves *disciples*, which means *learners*. Christianity is a teaching movement, with instruction from the Torah, the Psalms, the prophets, the apostles, and Christ himself—the consummate teacher. Correspondingly, Christianity is also a learning movement—in Christ we are *lifelong learners*. Brain function matters greatly to me not only as a pastor and teacher but also as a Christian. So here's "how exercise improves learning on three levels": "First, it optimizes your mind-set to improve alertness, attention, and

---

[3] Ratey, *Spark*, 4–5.

motivation; second, it prepares and encourages nerve cells to bind to one another, which is the cellular basis for logging in new information; and third, it spurs the development of new nerve cells."[4]

First, *mindset* is no small issue today in the age of digital distraction and dullness. If I can be *more alert* to the world, to others, and to mentally challenging texts and sequences of thought, then I'm interested. *Alertness* is a deeply Christian pursuit (and a key reason many of us make use of caffeine[5]). And in a day when so many are woefully and tragically distracted by unceasing devices and the mirage of multitasking, we could hardly list many more valuable benefits than *improved attention*.

Second and third, modest exertion of the body and persistence in it (say twenty-plus minutes[6]) produces a cascade of good effects in the brain and body, from neurogenesis (actually growing new brain cells) down to the nitty-gritty

---

4 Ratey, *Spark*, 53.

5 For a brief, Christian perspective on caffeine, see David Mathis, "God Caffeinated His World," Desiring God, April 25, 2019, https://www.desiringgod.org/.

6 Kelly McGonigal, *The Joy of Movement: How Exercise Helps Us Find Happiness, Hope, Connection, and Courage* (Avery, 2019), 18. As noted previously, McGonigal says the so-called runner's high is actually a "persistence high" from pushing the body past comfort level typically for twenty minutes or more.

strengthening of "the cellular basis for logging in new information."

So, active bodies improve learning. Exercise helps to develop new brain cells, encourages the binding of those cells, and improves our focus and eagerness to learn. Christians, of all people, would not want such discoveries to be lost on us.

## How It Works

Now, it's one thing to hear that moderate bodily exertion improves learning; it's another to hear specifically about three ways it does this; and it's another still to learn *how* it happens. Specifics like these motivate me, especially in those moments when I feel happy to stay sedentary and not take the uncomfortable step of overcoming the inertia of inactivity. How does it work? According to Ratey,

> Going for a run is like taking a little bit of Prozac and a little bit of Ritalin because, like the drugs, exercise elevates . . . neurotransmitters. It's a handy metaphor to get the point across, but the deeper explanation is that exercise balances neurotransmitters—along with the rest of the neurochemicals in the brain.[7]

7 Ratey, *Spark*, 38.

And we can go one step further:

> BDNF [Brain Deprived Neurotrophic Factor, which Ratey calls "Miracle Grow" for the brain] gathers in reserve pools near the synapses and is *unleashed when we get our blood pumping*. In the process, a number of hormones from the body are called into action to help. . . . During exercise, these factors push through the blood-brain barrier, a web of capillaries with tightly packed cells that screen out bulky intruders such as bacteria. . . . Once inside the brain, these factors work with BDNF to crank up the molecular machinery of learning. They are also produced within the brain and promote stem-cell division, especially during exercise. . . . The body was designed to be pushed, and in pushing our bodies we push our brains too.[8]

Make no mistake, the above observations are not explicitly *Christian*. At their best, they are in the realm of natural revelation. How, then, might we reflect as Christians on these

---

[8] Ratey, *Spark*, 51–53. As a Christian, I can't help but note that Ratey says "designed" in this last line: "The body was designed to be pushed." Elsewhere he says "built": "The human body is built for regular physical activity." Ratey, 68. The Harvard psychiatrist regularly makes his Darwinian assumptions explicit, but at times he can't help but stand in awe of the complexity of the human brain as the work of some designer or builder, not mere matter plus time plus chance.

fairly recent findings in neurology and their relationship to our God and his calling on us in Christ?

### Train the Body, Serve the Soul

"Bodily training is of some value," says Paul, even as he emphasizes that "godliness is of value in every way, as it holds promise for the present life and also for the life to come" (1 Tim. 4:8). *Some value* is a carefully crafted phrase. Doubtless, many in Paul's own day, as in ours, held the human body in too high regard. They needed to hear that bodily training is of *some* value but not too much. Yet others—perhaps especially Christians who had been awakened to the far greater value of holiness and life in the Spirit—needed to open their minds afresh to Paul's affirmation of *any* value at all.

Even as we affirm and seek to celebrate the far greater value of Christlikeness, we might ask ourselves, practically, What tangible *value* do I see and act on in bodily training? And for those of us who *do* find value in exercise, we might also ask, Do I simply want to lose fat, look better, and live longer in this fallen world? Or might I find a *value* in bodily training that *serves godliness* and (among other things) my brain function in the service of Christ?

Put another way, might my Christian life—my increasing godliness and Christlikeness—be compromised because I've failed to love my Lord *with all my mind*? In the words of John Piper, have I failed to "embrace serious thinking as a means of knowing and loving God and people"?[9] In this chapter, I am waving a little flag for you to consider, perhaps for the first time: how modest, regular exercise might be a means of building and conditioning *your brain* for serious thinking by improving mental energy, focus, clarity, and stamina. That is, *serious* thinking in the service of Christ and Christian joy.

In B. B. Warfield's famous essay "The Religious Life of Theological Students," he poses what seems to be an either-or dilemma for some: Should I study or should I pray? Warfield answers with a memorable both-and: How about "ten hours over your books, on your knees"?[10] Today, we might only add, "And how about after twenty minutes of persistent exercise?"

---

9 John Piper, *Think: The Life of the Mind and the Love of God* (Crossway, 2010), 179.
10 Reprinted in Benjamin B. Warfield, "The Religious Life of Theological Students," *Themelios* 24, no. 3 (1999): 31.

5

# For the Will

*Learn to Lean into the Hill*

I WONDER IF the apostle Paul might have been a runner.

Running is a curiously common theme in his sermons and letters. He refers to his own life and ministry as running (1 Cor. 9:26; Gal. 2:2; Phil. 2:16) and describes the Galatians' past faith in similar terms: "You were running well" (Gal. 5:7).

He also asks the Thessalonians to pray for him "that the word of the Lord may speed [run] ahead and be honored" (2 Thess. 3:1). He speaks of human effort and exertion (in contrast to divine mercy in election) as running (Rom. 9:16 NASB). He preached in Antioch about John the Baptist "finishing his course" (Acts 13:25), expressed to the Ephesian elders his desire that "I may finish my course" (Acts 20:24), and wrote in his final letter, "I have finished the race" (2 Tim. 4:7). In one of his most moving and memorable flourishes, he compares the heart of the Christian life to distance running: "Forgetting what lies behind and straining forward to what lies ahead, I press on toward the goal for the prize of the upward call of God in Christ Jesus" (Phil. 3:13–14).

While *walking* serves as his more common image of the Christian life (nearly thirty times in his letters), Paul's theology also had a place for speaking in more intense, even aggressive, terms—describing a kind of athletic capacity in the Christian life, as he wrote to the Corinthians: "Do you not know that in a race all the runners run, but only one receives the prize? So run that you may obtain it" (1 Cor. 9:24).

Whether or not Paul was a runner, many Christians (including me) have testified to finding the regular experience of pushing the body beyond comfort to be of more value than just physical health. Paul, after all, asserts that "bodily training is of some value," even as he emphasizes that "godliness is of value in every way" (1 Tim. 4:8). And bodily training is all the more valuable when it serves godliness—when lessons learned in pushing the body translate directly into the instincts of a healthy soul.[1]

[1] Robert Yarbrough comments on 1 Tim. 4:8: "Many who have been or are athletes . . . can testify that the enterprise of athletic training and competition has

## Exertion Produces Reward

Over time, I've discovered that pushing myself in exercise has served to strengthen my resolve, will, confidence, and eagerness to push myself elsewhere in life: in spiritual disciplines, as a husband and father, in difficult conversations, at work, and even around the house on evenings and weekends. Exercise teaches and reminds my body that *exertion produces reward*. There is often greater joy on the other side of greater work. Laziness may feel good for a moment, but it is not satisfying in the end. So I exercise to improve and sustain my work ethic.

In my last ten-plus years of exercising regularly, this strengthening of my will has been a surprising and significant benefit I did not expect. Overcoming my laziness toward exercise has helped me overcome other areas of laziness. Enjoying the benefits of bodily activity in exercise has helped condition me to lean into, rather than away from, bodily activity in all of life.

Exercise can train us to press through mild resistance in any difficult task and not quit—which is a priceless instinct to develop not just for life and work but also for the soul.

---

been a means of common grace that taught them a work ethic that might have never surfaced in them under the tutelage of church or academy alone." Robert Yarbrough, *The Letters to Timothy and Titus*, Pillar New Testament Commentary (Eerdmans, 2018), 45.

After getting in shape as a runner, I learned to push myself in various ways, such as "leaning into the hill."[2]

## Lean into the Hill

We each face our own hills each day. For some, it might begin with getting out of bed. Or initiating a conversation we expect to be difficult. Or starting into seemingly demanding work, schoolwork, or yard work. We all encounter hills; some more, some less. And when we're walking uphill, it takes more effort to keep putting one foot in front of the other. Again and again, we face challenges big and small. When they arise, what is our default mindset? Will we keep stepping? Slow down? Stop altogether? Or lean in?

---

[2] I could say more in this chapter related to handling stress and creating resilience, but let this footnote suffice for now. One of Ratey's chapters addresses stress. He refers to stress and our sedentary lifestyle as the twin killers of our day. We are more sedentary than ever and more stressed than ever. But exercise is remarkably effective at helping us gain resiliency in handling stress—not just emotionally but physically. Exercise "inoculates" us against stress: "Stress seems to have an effect on the brain similar to that of vaccines on the immune system. In limited doses, it causes brain cells to overcompensate and thus gird themselves against future demands. Neuroscientists call this phenomenon stress inoculation." John Ratey, *Spark: The Revolutionary New Science of Exercise and the Brain* (Little and Brown, 2008), 61. Exercise "fires up the recovery process in our muscles and our neurons. It leaves our bodies and minds stronger and more resilient, better able to handle future challenges, to think on our feet and adapt more easily." Ratey, 71.

## LEARN TO LEAN INTO THE HILL

Fellow runners might know the feeling. You're tired but continuing to strain toward the finish. You come upon a hill. The natural response is to slow down and slog through it. Stopping to walk feels tempting. But another mentality is to lean in and actually increase your effort. Push yourself to get over the hill and past it. Pummel your body for a purpose, as Paul did (1 Cor. 9:27). Expend more energy first. Get over the hill sooner, then enjoy the downslope.

Once a runner has learned what internal rewards lie on the other side of a hill, "leaning in" can become the new default, an instinct to develop in the rest of life—learning the reflex to press through resistance rather than immediately backing off.

### Develop the Instinct

It is deeply human to take the path of least resistance and avoid the hills in life we know we should be climbing each day. This is one reason we can be so easily distracted. It's not just our latest devices and the savvy attention merchants tricking us into distraction. Deep down we want to be distracted. Humans have craved and found distractions for centuries. The digital avenues for it have simply made distraction even easier. We typically want to avoid what we know we really should be doing because the hills that matter most are the hardest ones to climb.

Here's where physical training and exercise help not only the body but also the will. Physical exertion can help us develop the mentality to lean into tasks we resist instead of avoiding them and procrastinating—to "take resistance as a spur to action instead of avoidance."[3]

Instead of automatically slowing down or turning around when we come to a hill, we can *learn to lean in*. Learn to see the right hills as opportunities for fruitfulness, for what really matters, for genuine productivity on God's terms.

Today we are surrounded by a wealth of technologies that condition our souls and bodies to expect comfort and encourage our minds to intuitively calculate *easiest means* rather than *best outcomes*. Without intentionality, we will be shaped by our flesh's path of least resistance rather than the Spirit's call to bear fruit. If we don't take deliberate steps to rise above the increasingly low bars of discomfort in our society, we will be pulled down into the pit of lethargy around us. We will become (or remain) modern, soft, increasingly lazy, sedentary, and unproductive.

But in Christ, we have cause to move in another direction—to "not be conformed to this world, but be transformed by the renewal of [our minds]" (Rom. 12:2) through the renewal of our bodies—to present them as living sacrifices (12:1). When

[3] Mark Forster, *Get Everything Done: And Still Have Time to Play* (Hodder and Stoughton, 2000), 152.

in doubt, we don't want to default to what's easiest. We want to pursue what's most important, knowing that such things are typically the most mentally, emotionally, and physically demanding.

I mentioned above that the resolve, strength of will, and instinct to lean into resistance—rather than to quit—has not only served me at work but also at home. Exercise has helped me acquire a mentality to tackle tasks instead of to resist, procrastinate, and avoid. I want to develop the instinct that, when my wife asks me to carry some heavy boxes to the basement, I naturally jump on it rather than push it until later, that I get over the mental hurdle of doing more with my body, that I see movement as an opportunity and joy not a drawback and something to be avoided.

It is a great blessing to a household to have a husband and father who does not default to the couch, unwilling to move unless asked repeatedly. One who is gladly on his toes, ready to jump into constructive activity to bless his wife or children, to move the mundane and necessary tasks of the household forward and not let them pile up. And to do so eagerly with joy, not begrudgingly.

### Look to the Reward

One way to learn to lean into the hill is to learn to look to the reward. For the runner, the eyes of faith fuel us to press harder when we would rather slow down because we're looking beyond the hill in front of us. After a few more minutes, the hill will be behind me, and I will be happier for having leaned in rather than giving in.

The more we learn to look to the reward on the other side of the hill, the more—strange as it may seem at first—we learn to taste joy even on the uphill. Even now. The eyes of faith begin to *realize* or *taste* in seed form in the moment of hardship the joy that is to come. Faith is a tasting now in the present, despite its discomforts, of the full reward to come.

Whether Paul made a habit of running or not, he had learned how to lean in. When he met conflict in Philippi, he leaned in and bade the church to do so with him: "It has been granted to you that for the sake of Christ you should not only believe in him but also suffer for his sake, *engaged in the same conflict* that you saw I had and now hear that I still have" (Phil. 1:29–30). Resistance to the gospel challenged the apostle. But he didn't back down. He engaged. He leaned in. He continued to run and invited others to join him.

So too in Thessalonica. Conflict came; Paul leaned in. "Though we had already suffered and been shamefully treated at Philippi, as you know, we had boldness in our God to declare to you the gospel of God in the midst of much conflict" (1 Thess. 2:2). And yet, example though he is, Paul is not the supreme leaner.

## Jesus Leaned In

Jesus "set his face to go to Jerusalem" (Luke 9:51). Why? "For it cannot be that a prophet should perish away from Jerusalem" (Luke 13:33). This was emphatically not the easiest path. This was the hardest. The greatest of hills. He would *perish*, he said, and in the worst possible way: crucifixion.

When the author of Hebrews exhorts us to "run with endurance the race that is set before us" (Heb. 12:1), he also shows us how: "*looking to Jesus*, the founder and perfecter of our faith"—who leaned in, looking to the reward—"who for the joy that was set before him endured the cross, despising the shame, and is seated at the right hand of the throne of God" (12:2).

The resistance mentioned is not the one we might expect: shame. We cringe at the thought of the physical anguish of the cross. And we should; it was excruciating. And yet what Hebrews highlights here is not the physical pain, horrible as it was, but the shame. It was a public, prolonged, undignified execution at a crossroads. The unspeakable bodily pain of the cross would have been equaled, if not surpassed, by the utter shame.

Yet such pain *and shame* didn't send Jesus retreating. Rather, he looked through the obstacle, horrific as it was, and saw the reward on the other side of the shame. Even as such barriers were set immediately before his face, he looked to the joy on the far side: being seated at the right hand of his Father. And so he leaned into the hill.

6

# For Joy

*Seek Satisfaction in Him*

A DECADE AGO when I got serious again about running, it did not take me long to discover that when I exercise I'm happier today, not just later in life. I'm not deeply motivated by long-term health, but I am by today's joy. The long-term benefits of exercise are icing on the cake for me. What drives me is that I want to be joyful today. But that doesn't make it Christian—not until the joy of exercise serves joy in God. This brings us back to how exercise glorifies God.

## Exercise to Jumpstart Joy

Going back to Aristotle and to Hippocrates, the "father of medicine," in the fourth and fifth centuries before Christ, humans have long observed that we are happier when we're active and have been active. Hippocrates not only said, "Eating alone will not keep a man well; he also must take exercise,"[1] but he also treated depression with a long walk. And if that didn't seem to help right away, he advised taking another. "Walking is the best medicine."

God made our bodies to be healthier and happier when they move. As we saw in chapter 5, moving limbs increases our heart rate and circulates blood, transporting hormones and nutrients through the body—and especially to the brain—for optimal physical, mental, and emotional health. Without bodily movement and exertion, our brains don't get all the help they need to stay balanced and happy.

Even in the nineteenth century, prior to the great explosion of sedentary inventions in the twentieth, the famous English preacher Charles Spurgeon comments in his *Lectures to My Students* on the power of exercise to help human spirits: "A mouthful of sea air, or a stiff walk in the wind's face would not give grace to the soul, but it would yield oxygen to the body, which is next best."[2]

---

[1] Hippocrates, *Regimen I*, trans. W. H. S Jones, Loeb Classical Library (Harvard University Press, 1931), 4:229

[2] Charles H. Spurgeon, *Lectures to My Students* (Zondervan, 1954), 158.

Exercise alone will not create *spiritual* joy, but many Christians, including me, have found that it can help as a useful emotional boost. In the mysterious connection between body and spirit, food and sleep and exercise (or lack thereof) have the ability to lift (or drag down) our spiritual affections.

Rightly does pastor Mark Jones write for fellow pastors (and for all of us),

> Physical exertion is an important part of normal human life. . . . Overeating, as the fruit of a generally indulgent lifestyle, has become a tragically acceptable sin among many Christians in North America. I'm also equally persuaded that a lot of pastors should jump on a bike, go for a run, walk, or build some modest muscle, and they'd likely get more work done. A lack of discipline in areas such as food, exercise, and drink typically reflects a lack of discipline in other areas of the Christian life. . . . Exercise is a friend of the Christian, and one that, unless prohibited by health reasons, should be part of the ordinary Christian life.[3]

---

3 Mark Jones, "Remember the Body: The Pastor and His Exercise," Desiring God, June 20, 2019, https://www.desiringgod.org/. Jones concedes, "We know there are some people who have weight issues that are not simply a result of laziness and gluttony. Being large is not necessarily a sin. The human body is complex, and there may be other health factors at work that limit a person's ability to exercise. We should be careful not to judge too quickly, especially since poor eating can actually

## Glorify God by Enjoying Him

For more than twenty years, I have worked for Desiring God, a ministry in which one of the key truths for which we stand—and perhaps the most distinctive one—is that *enjoying God is essential to glorifying God as we ought.* To enjoy God is to glorify him. To be bored or uninterested in him is to dishonor him, whatever motions we go through with our bodies. And so, vital for our fulfilling the very purpose and calling of our lives is our enjoying, delighting in, and being satisfied with who God is for us in Christ.

For me, body stewardship stands or falls on whether it supports the pursuit of joy in God. The little bit of intense

---

be the result, in many instances, of socioeconomic factors." See also, Mark Jones, "Fit for Office," Desiring God, August 29, 2023, https://www.desiringgod.org/.

John Piper writes about "the correlation between the condition of the body and the condition of the soul" and that "consistent exercise has refining effects on our mental and emotional stability." And one of the motivations he points to is increased energy—in the service of doing good for others. John Piper, "Brothers, Bodily Training Is of Some Value," in *Brothers, We Are Not Professionals*, exp. ed. (B&H, 2013), 183, 185. In a book on church leadership, Paul Tripp writes about his newfound appreciation for stewarding the physical body. He realized, beginning with himself, that "widespread church and ministry leadership gluttony is robbing us of both gospel consistency and physical energy." He continues, "Regular exercise boosts and builds energy. Perhaps many of us are tired all the time not because of the rigorous demands of ministry but because of the lack of rigorous physical exercise in our normal routine. . . . [T]hese are not ancillary issues." Paul David Tripp, *Lead: 12 Gospel Principles for Leaders in the Church* (Crossway, 2020), 82.

exercise that I do is in its highest and best form about *enjoying God* and, so, glorifying him.

I am not motivated much by living longer. After all, "to depart and be with Christ . . . is far better" (Phil. 1:23). And I am not motivated much by looking fit and healthy. For me, those motivations are inadequate. My driving motivation under the banner of enjoying more of God is *the energy I get from expending energy*.

When I exercise regularly, I feel better. I feel like I can think clearer. I seem to sleep better. I'm generally happier. I don't know how much of it is the neurochemistry or other factors, including supernatural ones; but whatever it is, so far as I can tell, regular exercise puts my body and soul—and their mysterious relationship—into better position to clearly see and deeply savor who God is in Christ. As we saw in the last chapter, disciplining the body (1 Cor. 9:27) strengthens the will and chases away laziness in all of life. Regular exercise makes us more active, rather than passive or lazy, in every sphere and relationship—especially in relating to God through his word and prayer.

### Enjoy Him More Today

How might it change your exercise routine if you did not exercise for mere weight loss, long-term health, or improved physical appearance but instead to *enjoy God more today*? My plea in this book is for you to consider seriously how *physical* exertion can be a means, among others, of your *spiritual* health and joy.

God made our bodies with an enigmatic connection to our souls. How God stirs our souls in worship and Bible meditation often has tangible effects in our bodies. What we eat and drink, how much we sleep, and how we exert our physical bodies (or not) affect our level of contentment in the soul.

God not only means for us to enjoy the long-term benefits of regular bodily exertion but also the immediate effects that bolster and energize our emotions that day. And having our souls happy in God (with whatever little supplement we can get from exercise) is the premier way to fight and defeat the alluring lies of sin.

To be clear, the emotional boost of exercise (or at least avoiding the emotional drag of being sedentary) makes me more prepared to pursue and experience supernatural joy in God through his word, prayer, and Christian fellowship.

7

# For Love's Sake

*Get Fit for Good Works*

A FIFTH AND FINAL Christian motivation for exercise is the good of others. Or we could say, for love's sake. I exercise to make myself a better servant of others, to be *fit* for good works.

When my life is joyfully active and less sedentary, when I feel strong—when it seems clear to me that a happier life comes from activity, not passivity—I'm more ready to spring into action to help others. I'm ready to move. Ready to respond. Ready to hear. Ready to help. I believe that exercise makes me a better servant of others—a better husband, father, pastor, and friend.

Regular bodily exertion not only assists our personal pursuit of joy in God and fights against joy-destroying sin but also readies us to move beyond self-focus and have our hearts primed to meet the needs of others. Here's how John Piper explains why he has set aside time to exercise for more than fifty years:

> My main motive for exercise is purity and productivity. By purity, I mean being a more loving person (as Jesus said, "love your neighbor," Matthew 22:39). By productivity, I mean getting a lot done (as Paul said, "abounding in the work of the Lord," 1 Corinthians 15:58). . . . In short, I have one life to live for Jesus (2 Corinthians 5:15). I don't want to waste it. My approach is not mainly to lengthen it, but to maximize purity and productivity now.[1]

Precisely because "we are his workmanship, created in Christ Jesus for good works, which God prepared beforehand, that we should walk in them" (Eph. 2:10), we want to adequately condition our bodies so that they are a help, rather than a hindrance, in the daily cause of love. We want our bodies to be an aid—not an obstacle—in readying us to sacrifice our own comforts and energy to do good for others at home and for the church and beyond.

---

1 John Piper, "Brothers, Bodily Training Is of Some Value," in *Brothers, We Are Not Professionals*, exp. ed. (B&H, 2013), 186–87.

## Fit for What?

From this perspective, Christians can appreciate the term *fitness*. To call an active, able, healthy human body *fit* implies that the body is not an end in itself. The body's "fitness" is not for posing on camera or on stages but for *doing* something—accomplishing tasks in the world. The goal of fitness is not to look good in the mirror or on Instagram. True fitness serves other purposes. The body is *fit* to do something. The question is: *Fit for what?*

In Christ, we have far better answers to that question than secular workout culture and its false gods. Twice Paul uses a phrase that could be our rallying cry for a genuinely Christian call to fitness: "ready for every good work" (2 Tim. 2:21; Titus 3:1). In Christ, we want to cleanse our bodies "from what is dishonorable" (that is, from all forms of sin, including laziness) and "be a vessel for honorable use, set apart as holy, useful to the master of the house, *ready for every good work*" (2 Tim. 2:21).

We want to be ready. Ready to move and display God in his world. Ready with hands and arms, not too bulky and not too flabby, that can reach and lift and pull and push. Ready with feet and legs that feel life and energy in every step and spring with joy into blessing others. Ready with minds, hearts, and wills that typically would rather move than lounge, that would rather be active than sit and watch a screen for too long, that would rather work to help others than to calculate how to move as little as possible.

In the service of love, we want to get (and keep) our bodies, depending on our season of life, in the condition needed to serve God's callings on us to love others. We want to be the kind of people who desire to do good for others, knowing that such good often requires exerting our bodies in ways that are uncomfortable in the moment and even unthinkable if we are lazy and unfit.

As we have rehearsed many times, Paul says, "Glorify God in your body" (1 Cor. 6:20). But how does a body glorify God? One way to approach the question is through the lens of Matthew 5:16: "Let your light shine before others, so that they may see your good works and give glory to your Father who is in heaven." Invisible joy in God, in the inner person, overflows into visible, outward acts of love for the benefit of others (good works), accompanied by audible words that testify to the worth and value of God in Christ.

"Let your light shine" is what God's imagers do. They make the invisible God visibly present to human eyes in a particular place and time. What others see is our bodies doing good to bless others. And critical to God being glorified in our bodily actions is that our joy in him is made known in our faces, words, and manner. When our good works are seen (and heard) to be an overflow of our joy in God, he is glorified.

Not long ago, a friend and I were discussing the New Testament commands to love and good works. He commented, "Some of us imagine the Christian life as being sedentary, more about sitting than standing, more about talking and listening than anything causing exertion."

Although some may assume that life in Christ is lived mainly in living rooms and coffee shops, you don't get the impression that early Christians were sitting around all the time. They were active. Of course, we welcome the Lord's invitations (indeed commands!) to meditate, study, and be still in his presence. But we also encounter the teachings of Jesus, Peter, James, and Paul—one after another—sending us into gospel-informed, faith-fueled lives of meaningful activity.

## Devoted to Doing Good

As just a taste, consider more of what the apostle Paul had to say to his young associates Timothy and Titus. The rich in this present age, he writes, are not to sit on their wealth but to "do good, to be rich in good works, to be generous and ready to share" (1 Tim. 6:18). In his calling as a pastor, Titus is to be active, showing himself "in all respects to be a model of good works" (Titus 2:7). That is, don't be a model mainly by *what you don't do* but by the *good works you perform*—not to earn God's favor but as evidence of it so that you may extend it to others.

Paul expected both sound *words* and good *works* from his protégés. And he expected all Christians would be not just *willing* to do good but be "*zealous* for good works" (Titus 2:14). He wanted to ensure that those who profess faith are "careful to devote themselves to good works" (Titus 3:8). The problem with the false teachers in Crete was this: "They profess to know God, but they deny him by their works. They are detestable, disobedient, *unfit for any good work*" (Titus 1:16). Paul's instructions for Christians provide a conspicuous contrast: "Let our people learn to devote themselves to good works, so as to help cases of urgent need, and not be unfruitful" (Titus 3:14).

Particularly in our sedentary times, let us pray that the phrase the apostle crafted for Timothy and Titus would be true of us—that we would be "ready for every good work" (2 Tim. 2:21; Titus 3:1).

## Ready to Do Good

*Readiness to do good* may sound easy enough in theory, but practically it's a calling that our times can make difficult. In

GET FIT FOR GOOD WORKS

our world of flesh and blood—and now automobiles and screens—physical and emotional components accompany the spiritual in our readiness to do good. Christian good works begin in the soul, in hearts captured by Christ, in faith receiving his benefits, in desire to draw attention to him, in love wanting to do others good.

Then come these bodies. There's no way around them. Will they be barriers to doing good or *ready to act*? When needs arise, will our wills be primed to break the inertia of inactivity? When love calls, will our bodies be ready to move, step, bend, reach, lift, pull, and push? Will I be ready and willing to make use of this body God gave me, or have I cultivated a habit of heart to keep it on the shelf and use it as little as possible?

**Present Your Body**

God did not design and build our human bodies to be liabilities. They are precious gifts, crafted and sustained by God, to enable us to live and *do good* for his glory in our world. Letting your light shine before others to give glory to your Father in heaven (Matt. 5:16) involves your body.

Not only are our bodies "for the Lord" as we have seen but also "the Lord [is] for the body" (1 Cor. 6:13). God is pro-body, *for the body*; he's not anti-body, suspicious of bodies.

He gave his own Son a human body as a vessel for doing his will in the world.

So we too have bodies, prepared for us by our Father, to carry out his will in the world, doing good with our bodies to advance Christ's kingdom and glory in acts prompted by faith and with words that give meaning to our acts. We not only have negative actions to avoid but positive actions to pursue: "Glorify God in your body" (1 Cor. 6:20).

We are to *present our bodies* as living sacrifices (Rom. 12:1) and *present our members* not as instruments of sin but of righteousness (Rom. 6:13). Will that be active or sedentary? Most likely and most often, it will take some modest effort or exertion—sometimes vigorous. In the call of love, we must marshal our members and muscles to move around in the world with legs striding toward need and hands extending to help.

The question is not whether we Christians carry out our God-given calling in this physical world *in our bodies* but whether we will *be ready* to use them as each new day presents us fresh opportunities. Will we let our age condition our bodies to slow us down, to keep us still, to feel like liabilities rather than assets in the call of Christ?

Will you be "conformed to this world" with its sedentary defaults and endless screentime, letting it flatten your faith and calling? Or will you be "transformed by the renewal of your mind" so that you will not only be able to "discern what is the will of God" (Rom. 12:2) but also *be ready and able* to present your body to do it?

## Modest Upkeep

Lest we become deluded about the dignity of our bodies in this fallen age, we do well to remember C. S. Lewis's balancing word about "Brother Ass." Our bodies are "both pathetically and absurdly beautiful." They are "a useful, sturdy, lazy, obstinate, patient, lovable and infuriating beast; deserving now the stick and now a carrot."[2]

In Christ, we have stumbled on the treasure hidden in the field (Matt. 13:44). We now hold the pearl of great price (Matt. 13:45–46). We have tasted the surpassing worth of knowing Christ Jesus our Lord (Phil. 3:8). Enjoying *this life*, as the end, is pathetically small. Enjoying *Jesus* is a worthy, indeed vital, goal—now and forever. This is our life. He is our life.

And that enjoyment of Christ is sweetened by the regular use and modest upkeep of these bodies. God didn't make them to sit around only. He made them to meditate on his

---

2  C. S. Lewis, *The Four Loves* (1960; repr., Harcourt Brace, 1988), 101.

words, yes, and then to move into the world toward needs. Movement and exertion not only make us healthier and happier but also facilitate our calling to love. And in so loving, in the name of Jesus, our joy in him deepens and expands.

And *modest* upkeep will do the trick for most of us. Unlike our world and its extremes, we have a higher calling, flowing from the very purpose of God himself, to put Brother Ass to work in the service of love to the glory of God.

Conclusion

# Move the Needle

AT THE END OF THIS SHORT BOOK, I ask you to consider your default posture on life. That is, has your overall mindset become passive and sedentary, or do you expect and embrace regular activity and movement?

Do you think of your life as essentially stationary unless compelled by some great force into action? Or do you think of yourself as active, moving, working, often beckoned to stop or sit to address some particular task? Do you think of physical activity as an opportunity—to be happy, make others happy, and even draw fresh admiring attention to Christ?

Here's what I'd ask you to ponder: Might some change of your default mindset serve your spiritual joy, the glory of God, and the good of others? What if you sought to cultivate a new set of expectations for daily life and reorient your subconscious default from being passive to taking joy in the regular rhythms of sitting and moving, resting and vigorous activity?

If you have a passive and sedentary lifestyle, such a change may seem imponderable. Your energy level feels low, and you may think that means you need to do less, not more. But God made our marvelous bodies to expend energy to produce more energy. Perhaps your energy is low because you move so little. Maybe you need to expend what little energy you have in some good work, then rest, and so learn to increase your capacity. In this way, you can cultivate a new (and countercultural) mindset that movement, activity, work, exertion is not to be avoided as evil but, rather, embraced (in the power of the Spirit) as God's call on us for overcoming evil.

I encourage you to begin where you are with *small steps over the long haul*. Maybe it's just tracking your steps daily and setting a step goal for several weeks. Walking counts; it really does. Walk to increase your heart rate and push the nutrients and hormones your brain needs across the blood-brain barrier. Observe and remember how good it feels after you've expended yourself—as motivation for next time.

## Persist

In normal circumstances, your legs and feet will eventually become stronger. You will build up a base and cultivate a more active mindset, ready to use your body to help others—whether that involves going up and down stairs, taking out the trash, carrying boxes, washing dishes, wiping the counter, or picking up something off the floor. Serve others by embracing household chores with intentionality and purpose. Move with energy, and try to enjoy moving your body.

Know that the joy of movement grows over time. "Exercise is an acquired pleasure," writes Kelly McGonigal. "The joys of an activity reveal themselves slowly as the body and brain adapt."[1] Your body and brain are not fixed but pliable. God made them with a remarkable ability to change and develop if you stick with your activity. Your capacity for joy in exercise will grow—not just in weeks but months and years. Keep at it. Activating your body does become easier and more enjoyable as you persist.

### Joy Set Before Us

Most of us will be well served by *modest upkeep*, making subtle changes in our default mindset, and learning to enjoy exercise. Again, walking counts. It gets the blood pumping. Walking for thirty minutes, five times per week, will fulfill the recommendation of many experts. In time, thirty-minute

[1] Kelly McGonigal, *The Joy of Movement: How Exercise Helps Us Find Happiness, Hope, Connection, and Courage* (Avery, 2019), 43.

CONCLUSION

walks might become an acquired pleasure and, subsequently, you might enjoy lifting weights or even jogging. We tend to overestimate what can be done in the short run and underestimate what can be done in the long run.

In a world of sin and tragedy like ours, it is a wonder to have able hands, feet, and bodies. God made our bodies, the most remarkable objects in all of creation. And we are stewards of these priceless gifts that he designed and created and upholds for his glory, for our joy in him, and for the good of others through our acts of love.

"Bodily training" is indeed "of some value." And, godliness, all the more. So, as Christians, why not leverage some modest conditioning of our bodies in the service of Christlikeness? Why not seek to glorify God and magnify Christ *in* these bodies rather than *despite* them? Why not reorient fitness in our minds from looking good to doing good, to bless others through physically demanding acts of love? Why not condition our brains, strengthen our wills, and thicken our joy by leveraging what we can from these physical bodies in the pursuit of spiritual life and health?

So, as we're able, let's exercise our bodies for the conditioning and wellness of our souls and satisfaction in Christ, which glorifies him and overflows in love toward others.

# Acknowledgments

IN JANUARY OF 2017, I published one short, basic article at Desiring God on a Christian vision of exercise. I assumed that would be it. I moved on to other topics. But two years later, thanks to two friends—one old, another new—I felt the need to say more.

First, the longtime friend, Justin Taylor at Crossway Books, dreamed up this book for me and even pitched it from the beginning as *A Little Theology of Exercise*. The title is a play on Helmut Thielke's *A Little Exercise for Young Theologians*. (I take it that Justin thinks some young theologians could use a little exercise!) The concept resonated. The book idea stuck.

Just a few months later, the new friend, David Bush in Des Moines, contacted me about speaking at the Inspire Conference, a Christian event on fitness and exercise. I was surprised but intrigued by the invitation for a pastor to speak on exercise, and I was willing to make the short trip south

ACKNOWLEDGMENTS

to Iowa to give it a try. When David asked for a title, I gave him Justin's: "A Little Theology of Exercise." The Inspire event happened in January of 2020. Both preparing for it and experiencing it inspired me that more could be said—by a pastor about exercise—than I first thought.

So, thank you, Justin and David, for pulling at this cord and drawing more out of me on this topic in these eight years. And thank you to the whole team at Crossway—such a pleasure to work with—from the earliest stages all the way through. Thanks especially to Chris Cowan who served as editor and made so many good suggestions.

Thank you also to my colleagues (and dear brothers) at Desiring God who encouraged me to keep speaking and writing (here and there, not too much!) about exercise from a Christian Hedonistic point of view. Much of the content of this book I first shared in public messages at Inspire, or in chapel at Bethlehem College and Seminary, or in various articles at Desiring God over the last eight years. In particular, Marshall Segal, Scott Hubbard, and Greg Morse had their hands in this work through edits and input year after year. Also, John Piper and Jon Bloom were significant encouragers along the way as men who themselves have lived this vision of putting bodily training into the service of godliness—and joy. To them, I've dedicated this book.

## ACKNOWLEDGMENTS

Thank you also to my brother pastors at Cities Church. The ten years of our church life together has overlapped almost totally with my coming freshly alive to the value of bodily training, in the pursuit of spiritual joy, and getting my body active again. Our team of pastors is a physically active and spiritually mature band of brothers who have encouraged this vision and substantiated it.

Finally, I thank my wife, Megan, and our four children. In the challenges and joys of this book coming into being, the writing was nothing. It was all the exercising. In ten years, Megan's seen the worst (and I hope some best) of a husband who tries to shoehorn workouts into the busy life of a young family. I have made many misteps and caused frustration. I believe the spiritual discipline of physical exercise can make a man better, but it can also create inconveniences for his family. This project only had legs when Megan gave her blessing. I pray that over time she and our children will feel a clear sense of appreciation for having a husband and father who was happier, stronger, more energetic, and more eager to serve the family with his body because of some exercise.

Actually, though, *his body*? I am not my own. I was bought with a price. Thank you, Jesus, for a wife and children and church and coworkers and friends—and for this "useful, sturdy, lazy, obstinate, patient, lovable, and infuriating beast." You made it and gave it and sustain it—for my joy, the good of others, and your glory. What a privilege and pleasure, even now, in this sin-sick and cursed world, to marvel at your person and grace and to seek to magnify you in my body.

# General Index

acquired pleasure, 95–96
action, 72
activity, 83, 87, 93
Adam, 11, 21n1, 25, 36
ADHD, 58
aerobic exercise, 46
alertness, 60–61
animals, 4, 6
Aristotle, 77
athletes, 5, 58, 68–69n1
attention, 60–61
avoidance, 72

bodily movement, 2, 11, 33, 57, 78. *See also* movement
bodily training, 16–17, 31–32, 64, 68, 96
body
  as glorifying God, ix–xiii, 30–34
  as living sacrifices, 33, 52, 72, 89–91
  resurrection of, 8, 34–37
  as temple of the Holy Spirit, 22–23, 29–30
brain, 6, 46, 58–60, 63n8, 65
Brain Deprived Neurotrophic Factor (BDNF), 63

caffeine, 61
cannabis, 47
*Chariots of Fire* (film), 45–46
Christian Hedonism, x–xiii, 48
Christian life, 2, 10, 20, 31, 64–65, 68, 79
Christianity, 60
Christians, xii, xiii, 10, 23–24, 33, 54, 60, 88
Christlikeness, 32n2, 42, 49, 64, 96
complementarity, 21n1
computer, 2
conflict, 74

## GENERAL INDEX

consecration, 19, 39
contentment, 48, 82
creation, 22, 96
curse, 24–26, 28

da Vinci, Leonardo, 7
Darwinism, 63n8
death, 24–25, 28, 34
depression, 78
Desiring God, 80
diet, x, xi, 2, 9, 11, 16, 53, 79
disability, 26–27, 36, 52
discipline, 1, 33, 41, 69, 79, 81
distance running, 7, 67–68
dopamine, 46

emotions, 13, 54, 78, 79, 82
endocannabinoids, 46–47
endogenous morphine, 46
endorphins, 46, 47
endurance running, 4, 75
energy, 94
engineering, 7
Eve, 11, 21n1
evolution, 63n8
exercise
  as acquired pleasure, 95–96
  and the brain, 58–60
  and emotions, 79
  as a gift, 39–41
  as holy, 15–18
  as inoculating stress, 70n2
  and learning, 60–62
exertion, 13, 20, 32, 33, 69–70, 82

faith, 13, 28, 32n2, 41, 42–43, 73–74, 88, 90
fatness, 9n10, 11, 12
feet, 6–7, 8, 53, 85, 94, 96
female, 21n1
fitness, xiii, 16, 17, 85–87, 96
fitness community, 21n1, 23
food, x, xi, 2, 9, 11, 16, 53, 79
Francis of Assisi, ix-x

glory, 8, 14, 23, 30–34
gluttony, 79n3
God
  asking for help, 41–42
  as commending exertion, 31–32
  creative design of, 35
  enjoying of, 80–82, 91–92
  existence of, 8
  glory of, 8, 14, 23, 27, 30–34, 48, 55, 77, 80–81, 96
  as maker of bodies, 21–24
godliness, 32n2, 42, 64, 68
good works, 83, 84, 85, 87, 88, 89
gospel, 74, 80n3, 87
gratitude, 39–41, 43

habits of grace, 1, 4
hands, 8, 11, 53, 85, 90, 96
happiness, 48, 54, 77–78
Hartmann, Gerard, 7
health, 32–34
Heidelberg Catechism, xii

# GENERAL INDEX

hell, 25
hills, 70–71, 75
Hippocrates, 77–78
holiness, 15–18, 32n2, 64
Holy Spirit
  fullness of, 35
  indwelling of, 29–30
  power of, 94
household tasks, 73, 95
human anatomy, ix–xiii, 4
human nature, 9
humanity, embracing of, 3–4
humiliation, 34, 37

image of God, 21n1, 24, 51–52, 54, 86
inactivity, 12, 62, 89
incarnation, 28
industrial revolution, 2, 13
Instagram, 85
intentionality, 72, 95
internet, 2

Jesus Christ
  body of, 28
  enjoying of, 91–92
  humiliation of, 34
  as image of God, 54–55
  as leaning in, 75–76
  life of, 53–54
  second coming of, 35–36
  walking of, 12, 53
Jones, Mark, 79–80n3
joy, 2, 14, 27, 48, 65, 73, 82, 95

laziness, 31, 41, 69, 79n3, 81, 85
learning, 60–62
Lewis, C. S., ix–xi, 91
Liddell, Eric, 45–46
Lieberman, Daniel, 17n1
living sacrifices, 33, 52, 72, 89–91
love, 83, 84, 86, 90

McDougall, Christopher, 4, 7
McGonigal, Kelly, 47, 48n5, 61n6, 95
male, 21n1
marijuana, 47
marriage, 16, 17
mental clarity, 58
mental labor, 57
mind, 13, 24, 72, 85–86, 96
mindset, 61, 70, 93, 94–95
modern diet, 2, 9
modest upkeep, 91–92, 95
morphine, 46, 47
motivation, 49, 60–61, 81
movement
  and the brain, 60
  and happiness, 48
  wonder of, 4–6

natural revelation, 63–64
neo-pagans, x
neurogenesis, 61
neurotransmitters, 62
new heavens and new earth, 36–37
Newton, Isaac, 8

obesity, 9n10, 11, 12
oxytocin, 46

parable of the talents, 55
passivity, 33–34, 81, 83, 93–94
Paul
  on bodily training, 64
  on good works, 85
  on honoring Christ, 52
  on leaning in, 74
  missionary journeys of, 12, 53
  proteges of, 87–88
  on running, 67–68
persistence, 94–95
persistence high, 48n5
personal computer, 2
physiology, 4
Piper, John, 65, 80n3, 84
pleasure, 16, 45, 48, 95–96
prayer, 20, 39, 41–42
priorities, 3–4
procrastination, 73
productivity, 72, 84
purity, 84

Raichlen, David, 47
Ratey, John, 4–5, 6, 58–60, 62–63, 70n2
rebellion, 19, 25
redemptive story, 20
resilience, 70n2
resistance, 72–73, 74, 75

resurrection bodies, 8, 34–37
reward, 48, 69–70, 73–74
righteousness, 90
runner's high, 46, 47, 61n6
running, 7, 67–68, 70, 77, 96
Ryle, J. C., 33–34

salvation, 51
Scripture, bodily motion in, 10–12, 23, 28
sedentariness, 2, 3, 8–10, 13, 32, 53, 54, 57, 62, 70n2, 87, 93
serotonin, 46
shame, 75–76
sin, 24–27, 28, 30, 79n3, 85, 90, 96
smartphone, 2
soul, 32–34, 68, 82
spiritual body, 35
spiritual disciplines, 1, 69
spiritual health, 32–34, 82
spiritualism, 32
Spurgeon, Charles, 78
stewardship, xii, 80
stress, 47, 59, 70n2
sugar, xi, 9n10

teaching, 60
technology, 2, 9, 72
television, 2, 5
thanksgiving, 17, 39–41
Tripp, Paul, 80n3

unbelievers, 14, 43

vigorous aerobic exercise, 46

walking, 68, 94, 95–96
Warfield, B. B., 65

will, 13, 69, 73, 81
word of God, 16, 17, 19–20, 39, 43, 67
work ethic, 69

Yarbrough, Robert, 68–69n1

# Scripture Index

*Genesis*
1:27 .........51, 54
2:7...........21n1
2:22 .........21n1

*Deuteronomy*
31:20.........12
32:15.........12

*Judges*
3:17 ..........11
3:22 ..........11

*1 Samuel*
4:18 ..........11

*Psalms*.......
18..............11
19:1 ..........22
40..............28
40:6–8 .......28, 52
139:13–14..21
139:14 ......xi

*Proverbs*
21:25.........31

*Isaiah*
53:3 ..........53

*Jeremiah*
5:28 ..........12

*Matthew*
5:16 ..........86, 89
5:29 ..........25
5:30 ..........25
10:28.........25
13:44.........91
13:45–46 ...91
22:39.........84
28:19–20 ...7

*Luke*
9:51 ..........75
13:33.........75

*John*
1:14 ..........54
17:4 ..........53
17:6 ..........53
17:26.........53

*Acts*
13:25.........67
20:24.........67

*Romans*
1:20 ..........22
1:21 ..........40
1:24 ..........25
6:6.............24
6:12 ..........25, 33
6:13 ..........90

## SCRIPTURE INDEX

7:4............28
7:24..........24
8:9–11........29
8:10..........24
8:11..........25
8:13..........30
8:20–23.......25
9:16..........67
12:1..........33, 52, 72, 90
12:2..........52, 72, 91

*1 Corinthians*
1:18–29.......27
6:13..........24, 31, 35, 89
6:14..........35
6:19..........29
6:19–20.......vi, 22, 23, 30, 40
6:20..........27, 86, 90
9:24..........68
9:26..........67
9:27..........33, 41, 71, 81
10:16.........28
10:31.........23, 55
11:24.........28
11:27.........28
11:29.........28

15:42–44......35
15:49.........36
15:58.........84

*2 Corinthians*
4:4...........53, 54
4:16..........8
5:10..........25
5:15..........84
12:9..........26

*Galatians*
2:2...........67
5:7...........67
5:23..........41

*Ephesians*
2:10..........84
4:28..........31

*Philippians*
1:20..........30, 52
1:23..........81
1:29–30.......74
2:8...........28
2:12..........29
2:16..........67
3:8...........91
3:13–14.......68
3:21..........34

*Colossians*
1:15..........53, 54
3:17..........24

*1 Thessalonians*
2:2...........74
5:23..........33

*2 Thessalonians*
3:1...........67
3:10..........31
3:11..........31

*1 Timothy*
2:12–13.......21n1
3:16..........32n2
4.............16
4:1–5.........16
4:4...........40
4:4–5.........17, 39
4:5...........19, 39
4:7...........32n2
4:8...........2, 16, 31, 32, 64, 68, 68n1
6:3...........32n2
6:11..........32n2
6:18..........87

*2 Timothy*
2:6...........31
2:21..........85, 88
4:7...........68

## SCRIPTURE INDEX

*Titus*
1:1 . . . . . . . . . . .32n2
1:16 . . . . . . . . .88
2:7 . . . . . . . . . . .88
2:14 . . . . . . . . .88
3:1 . . . . . . . . . . .85, 88
3:8 . . . . . . . . . . .88
3:14 . . . . . . . . .88

*Hebrews*
10:5 . . . . . . . . .28
10:5–7 . . . . . .52
10:7 . . . . . . . . .28
10:10 . . . . . . . .28
12:1 . . . . . . . . .75
12:2 . . . . . . . . .75

*1 Peter*
2:24 . . . . . . . . .28, 52

*2 Peter*
1:5–7 . . . . . . . .32n2
3:11 . . . . . . . . .32n2
3:18 . . . . . . . . .2

# ❉ desiringGod

Everyone wants to be happy. Our website was born and built for happiness. We want people everywhere to understand, embrace, and apply the truth that *God is most glorified in us when we are most satisfied in him*. We provide a daily stream of new written, audio, and video resources to help you find truth, purpose, and satisfaction that never end. We've also collected more than forty years of John Piper's speaking and writing, including translations into almost fifty languages. And it's all available free of charge, thanks to the generosity of those who've been blessed by the ministry.

If you want more resources for true happiness, or if you want to learn more about our work at Desiring God, we invite you to visit us at desiringGod.org.

**desiringGod.org**

# Also Available from David Mathis

**FOREWORD BY JOHN PIPER**

*habits of grace*

david mathis

Enjoying Jesus through the Spiritual Disciplines

This book explores how Bible reading, prayer, and fellowship with other Christians—three foundational "habits of grace"—have the power to awaken our souls to God's glory and stir our hearts for joyful service.

For more information, visit **crossway.org**.